THE MOREHOUSE MYSTIQUE

Lessons to Develop Black Men

John H. Eaves, Ph.D.

African American Images

JUN 2009

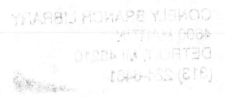

First Edition, First Printing

Front cover illustration by Harold Carr, Jr.

Copyright © 2009 by John H. Eaves, Ph.D.

Printed in the United States of America

10-Digit ISBN #: 1-934155-14-4
13-Digit ISBN #: 978-1-934155-14-1

JUN 2009

Dedication

This book is dedicated to the memory of my father, Dr. John H. Eaves, Sr. (class of 1952), who always believed in me, always encouraged me to seek academic excellence and, even in death, continues to be a source of inspiration.

Table of Contents

Acknowledgements

The completion of this book would not have been possible without the support, encouragement, and assistance of family members, friends, and associates. I wish to thank my family, including my mother, Evelyn; my children, Isaac and Keturah; my sisters, Martha and Marian; and a host of relatives as well as some of my closest Morehouse classmates, Mark B. Lewis (class of 1984), Vernon Comer (class of 1984), Dr. Kevin McCowan (class of 1985), and Rev. Darryl Canady (class of 1988).

Second, I wish to thank my friends and associates at Morehouse College who gave me much needed moral and technical support. These individuals include: Alvin "Skip" Darden (class of 1972), Dean of Freshmen; Dr. Walter Earl Fluker, Executive Director of the Leadership Center; Henry Goodgame (class of 1984), Director of Alumni Affairs; Adrienne Harris, former Associate Vice President for Executive Communications; Kai Jackson Issa, Managing Editor of the Reverend Howard Thurman Papers; Rev. Herman "Skip" Mason, College Archivist and Interim Vice President for Student Services/Dean of Students; Dr. Kevin Rome (class of 1989), former Vice President for Student Services/Dean of Students; Julie Tongue, Office of Communications; and countless others within the Morehouse community who supported this project.

I would also like to acknowledge the wonderful cooperation of the Auburn Avenue Research Library on African American Culture and History, Atlanta-Fulton County Library System, and the Robert W. Woodruff Library, Atlanta University Center.

Finally, I wish to thank my many friends who provided me with unexpected and unselfish support. Among these are Dr. Sheila T. Gregory, Associate Professor of Higher Education and Educational Leadership at Clark Atlanta University, and Dr. Carey Wynn (class of 1970), my freshman year history professor who, through Divine intervention, contacted me at the 11th hour of this project, provided technical guidance and historical insights, and affirmed my belief that God sends guardian angels to keep "charge over thee" when in need.

Preface: Why I Wrote This Book

I am a second generation Morehouse Man (class of 1984).

Going to Morehouse College is an Eaves family tradition. I followed in the footsteps of my father, Dr. John H. Eaves, Sr. (class of 1952). I am the ninth of 12 extended family members—uncles, cousins, and nephews—who attended Morehouse.

While growing up, I heard my father and uncles boast about the greatness of Morehouse. They talked about their interactions with the legendary Morehouse College president, Dr. Benjamin Elijah Mays, and the dynamic speeches they heard during daily Chapel in Sale Hall. They talked about the strong bonds they forged with their Morehouse classmates.

Most importantly, they shared what it meant to be a Morehouse Man. A Morehouse Man, they said, was academically prepared, well rounded, intelligent, respectful of women, and committed to excellence.

When I was a senior at Raines High School in Jacksonville, Florida, I applied to only one college: Morehouse.

My excitement about attending Morehouse increased when, during the summer following high school graduation, I received my dormitory assignment in the mail. I talked to Morehouse students who spoke positively about their experiences, and I envisioned what it might be like to enter the sacred halls of this great institution. Finally, on August 18, 1979, my parents and my paternal grandfather drove me to the Jacksonville International Airport to catch a flight to Atlanta. As I boarded the plane, my grandfather extended his blessings, and my mother gave me a hug and kiss. My father told me to uphold the family tradition of academic excellence. He told me to make him proud, and to not bring shame to the family name.

With mixed emotions, I bade farewell, for I was leaving the comforts of home to begin the journey towards becoming a Morehouse Man. Never did I have second thoughts about that decision, and it was a decision that changed my life.

My life as a Morehouse student was one of intensive growth. I was motivated by my peers, who were some of the brightest and most ambitious young men I had ever met. My professors were some of the most brilliant scholars in the world, and they challenged me to excel. I honed my leadership skills through my participation on the football team, the Student Government Association, and various community service activities. I was inspired by dynamic speeches at the weekly college assemblies given by President Hugh M. Gloster, famous politicians, national celebrities, and community activists, including President Jimmy Carter, Atlanta Mayor Maynard Jackson, Rev. Jesse Jackson, Rev. Martin L. King, Sr., actor Sidney Portier, United Nations Ambassador Andrew Young, actress Jane Kennedy, and Miss America, Vanessa Williams.

My fondest Morehouse memory, however, occurred in March of 1982, when I attended a community event in Atlanta honoring Dr. Benjamin Mays. Following the event, my Uncle Emmanuel Eaves (class of 1949) introduced me to the great man. Looking at me intently, Dr. Mays asked, "Young man, how are your grades?" I was embarrassed by his question because I was not doing well academically at the time. Although brief, that two-minute exchange challenged and motivated me to reach my full potential as a Morehouse student.

My Morehouse experience transformed me. I entered college as a naive 17-year-old freshman with shaky confidence. I didn't know what I wanted to do with my life, professionally or personally. When I graduated in 1984, however, I was a confident man and felt the world was mine to conquer. Several years later, in 1991, I enrolled at the University of South Carolina as a doctoral student in the educational leadership program. At the time, there was much concern about the plight of African American males in American society. According to a disturbing report released in 1992, more African American men were in prison than enrolled in college. This startling revelation piqued my interest in the status of African American males in higher education. I began to ponder why such a disproportionate number of young African American males did not seek higher education. Why weren't more African American males productive academically? Compared to African American females and males of other races, ethnicities, and nationalities, the achievement gap was abysmal. I began to reflect on my days as a Morehouse student, when I was first introduced to the "Morehouse Mystique." I had both experienced and witnessed how this mystique transformed boys who lacked focus or purpose into men who went on to make significant contributions to American society.

Former Morehouse president Dr. Benjamin Mays said, "…there is an intangible something at Morehouse College. If it is ever lost, Morehouse will be just like any other college…."[1] The mystique is based partly on Morehouse's exclusive status as the only all-male, predominately Black college within the American system of higher education. Jacqueline Fleming in her book, *Blacks in College* noted that Morehouse "sacrifices many of the frills in favor of developing

a well-rounded masculine orientation to future attainment."[2]
She stated further: "While students perceive general cognitive
growth…it is clear that any gains are strictly in the service of
career and leadership development."[3]

From September 1997 to May 2008, I conducted
research at Morehouse College to determine the secret of the
college's success at graduating so many top quality students.
I discovered there is indeed a transformative effect. Based on
the college's rich tradition and heritage, a culture of excellence
and high expectations inspires students to mature as men and
achieve academically. Together, outstanding African American
students and leading role models in education, business,
ministry, science and technology, government service, and the
arts motivate students to set and achieve goals and to become
problem-solvers for society. Few institutions provide the type
of compelling learning environment for African American
males as Morehouse. That's why, given the low enrollment
of African American males in higher education, this is a story
that must be told.

Significance of This Book

Although Morehouse is an ideal site to examine issues
involving African American male students, the college is rarely
studied. This book is the most comprehensive study of the
institutional culture of Morehouse College and its effect on
leadership development. Most research studies on single-sex
colleges have focused on female institutions.[4] Only a few
studies have dealt with male, single-sex institutions.[5] Even
fewer studies have examined single-sex, predominantly Black
male institutions.[6] Therefore, the results revealed within this
book will add new information to our knowledge about the

effectiveness of single-sex institutions as well as African American male student leadership development within higher education. Using Morehouse as a case study will shed light on the institutional factors that inspire African American males to learn and become leaders.

This book is targeted to all who counsel, mentor, and teach African American male students.

Dr. John H. Eaves
Author
Class of 1984

Introduction: The Morehouse Mystique

"Morehouse College has replenished the earth with what is becoming an endangered species and that is the educated African American male."[7]

Dr. Charles J. McDonald
Professor, Brown University Medical School

Morehouse College, a predominantly Black all-male college, is the only institution of its kind in the United States. Since its inception in 1867, Morehouse College has amassed a remarkable track record of producing leaders in various professional fields—more African American male doctors, lawyers, scientists, judges, engineers, theologians, and educators than any other American college. Five percent of all African Americans with a Ph.D. are Morehouse graduates,[8] and more African American male medical students graduated from Morehouse than any other college in the United States.[9] Additionally, Morehouse College is lauded as one of the country's top producers of African American male graduates with degrees in biology, the humanities, mathematics, and health science fields.[10]

Top College for African American Men

Morehouse College is a highly selective institution, with an enrollment of approximately 2,800 students. It has been consistently rated as one of the leading liberal arts colleges in the nation by *U.S. News and World Report*. Among a survey of 2,000 African American college presidents, chancellors, and provosts Morehouse was rated as having "a good social and educational environment for African Americans."[11] In 2007, *Newsweek/Kaplan* named Morehouse the "hottest male college in the nation" and in 2008, the *Princeton Review* named the college as one of the best learning centers in the Southeast.[12]

Morehouse College is accredited by the Commission on Colleges of the Southern Association of Colleges and Schools. It is one of five historically Black colleges and universities with a Phi Beta Kappa National Honor Society chapter, the nation's oldest and largest academic honor society. *The Wall Street Journal* ranked Morehouse 29th among the top 50 most successful schools in the country that sends students to prestigious graduate school programs;[13] of these top 50 schools, Morehouse is the only Black college. Morehouse graduates are also enrolled at 13 of the top 15 graduate and professional schools. Since 1994, Morehouse has produced three Rhodes Scholars (one of only two Black colleges to do so). In recent years, it has produced two Fulbright Scholars, three Luce Scholars, and two Marshall Scholars. Ten to 15 of its graduates consistently enroll in the Harvard Business School. Of the 547-member class of 2007, at least 16 Morehouse Men are pursuing graduate and professional degrees at Harvard University.

Nationally Renowned Leaders

As one of three all-male liberal arts colleges in the United States, Morehouse has the distinction of being the only one that is predominantly African American. Each year, Morehouse consistently produces 500 African American male graduates.

During its history, the international reputation and influence of Morehouse has grown immeasurably, and this reputation is largely due to its prominent alumni. Some of the more well-known graduates include: theologian Dr. Howard Thurman (class of 1923); Nobel Peace Prize Laureate, Dr. Martin Luther King, Jr. (class of 1948); former U.S. Health and Human Services Secretary, Dr. Louis Sullivan (class of 1954); former Mayor of Atlanta, Georgia, Maynard Jackson (class of 1956); former U.S. Surgeon General, Dr. David Satcher (class of 1963); civil rights activist and Chairman of the Board of the NAACP, Julian Bond (class of 1971); Academy Award winning actor, Samuel L. Jackson (class of 1972); three-time U.S. Olympian, Edwin Moses (class of 1978); and actor and award winning filmmaker, Spike Lee (class of 1979).

Success Despite Societal Challenges

The success of Morehouse College is astounding in light of historical and contemporary societal issues that have confronted African American males. From the Reconstruction era following the Civil War to the 1950s, African American males, particularly in the South, endured threats of lynching, attended segregated schools, experienced housing and employment discrimination, and have died disproportionately on the battlefield since World War I. These challenges undermined males' pursuit of higher education more so than African American females. For example, from 1900 to 1940, fewer African American males than females attended college, although more African American males graduated. After 1940, African American female college entrance rates continued to exceed that of males, and their graduation rates have been higher than males as well.[14]

From the 1980s to the present, an unprecedented amount of media attention has been given to the plight of African American males. African American males are disproportionately incarcerated, unemployed, victimized by crime, and inclined to suffer premature deaths. Education is devalued in the eyes of many young African American males who consider academic achievement as "acting white," not "cool," or not "macho." However, educational success is the key to reversing these disparities and providing social mobility and economic stability for African American males.[15] Many studies affirm that progress along the primary-to-graduate-school pipeline offers males a greater chance of enjoying professional success, economic security, and personal well-being.

Clearly, based on the disparate statistics, most colleges and universities have failed to meet the learning and developmental needs of African American male students. Recruitment, retention, and graduation of Black males must become a top priority. By studying Morehouse, we can begin to understand one powerful approach to inspiring academic achievement and leadership development of African American male students.

Formula of Success

While every educational institution has its own unique learning environment, Morehouse College has a distinctive culture of traditions, rituals, norms, and ceremonies—the Morehouse Mystique—that evolved over its history of more than 140 years.

Over the years, many have attempted to explain the mystery behind Morehouse's success. An official Morehouse publication describes the mystique as follows:

"...the will to strive for excellence and to make the difference. It's a sense of your own humanity. It's about caring for your brothers and sisters, whoever they may be. From your first hours on campus, your first days, your first semester, you will begin to discover what it means to be a Man of Morehouse. You will feel the pride and the sense of responsibility. You will know."[16]

Former Morehouse College president, Dr. Leroy Keith (class of 1961), described the Morehouse Mystique "as a patented mixture of maxims, myths and images, brewed in a climate of tough love."[17] Others have described the Morehouse Mystique as follows: the courage and self-confidence the college instills in its students;[18] the leadership principles Morehouse students are required to follow;[19] and the emphasis on character building and cultural development.[20] The definitions of the mystique may differ, but the fact remains that Morehouse College enjoys unparalleled success in inspiring students to learn and lead, and this book will provide insight into how Morehouse achieves its mission.

How This Book Is Divided

This book uncloaks the mystery of the Morehouse Mystique by providing an historical and contemporary analysis of the institutional culture of Morehouse College. Part 1 provides a chronological review of the Morehouse Mystique, tracing its origins from the college's early days through 1968. Part 2 provides an analysis of the Morehouse Mystique, reviews the current state of African American males in education, outlines the lessons that can be extrapolated and applied to other educational institutions for the comprehensive development of African American males and describes the distinctive traditions, events, and ceremonies that take place on the Morehouse campus today. The book concludes with perspectives that are shared by the Morehouse administration, faculty, staff, and students and the impact of the "mystique" upon academic achievement and leadership development.

PART 1

A Rich Legacy of Leadership

Dr. Benjamin Elijah Mays
Morehouse College President, 1940-1967
Chapter 1: The Founding Fathers and
Early Presidents Era (1867–1906)

Chapter 1: The Founding Fathers and Early Presidents Era (1867–1906)

"Morehouse College, since its humble inauspicious beginnings...has been dedicated to the task of building men: first by enlightening their minds then by freeing them from the shackles of a psychological conditioning brought about by nearly two hundred years of slavery. "[21]

Dr. Edward Jones
Morehouse Professor and College Historian

Morehouse College was founded with the seemingly impractical idea of educating African American men for leadership roles during an era in American history when the newly emancipated people of the South were universally considered intellectually inferior. African American males in particular were portrayed as socially and morally depraved. Yet, whites and African Americans of goodwill came together, defied the popular opinion of the day, and founded a school in 1867 that today has graduated more African American men with baccalaureate degrees than any other American college or university. This is a noteworthy achievement, given the historical record of physical violence, inferior schooling, public lynching, racial stereotyping, and economic challenges that have afflicted African American males in their pursuit of education in the United States.

To appreciate the significance of Morehouse and its legacy of leadership, we will trace the college's fortuitous historical developments during the first 100 years that created a truly distinctive culture espousing scholarship and leadership. This journey involved several name changes, the relocation of the school from Augusta, Georgia, to its current site in Atlanta, and the evolution of the school from a one-room schoolhouse to a college of international acclaim.

Some of the emerging factors that facilitated the institution's ability to fulfill its mission include: the unrelenting determination of the founding fathers and early presidents to establish an educational institution during challenging political, social, and economic times in the South; the bold, visionary presidential leadership of Dr. John Hope and Dr. Benjamin Mays, who raised the institution into national acclaim and left indelible marks on the minds and hearts of young African American men; the cadre of dedicated faculty that trained the minds of students and inspired their career aspirations; and a zealous student body that has had, since its beginning, an eagerness to learn and to positively impact society.

Augusta Institute

Originally named Augusta Institute, Morehouse College was founded in 1867 in Augusta, a city located in the rural, eastern part of Georgia. Augusta Institute was a theological school for "colored" Baptist ministers.

Three men played important roles leading to the founding of Augusta Institute: the Rev. Richard C. Coulter, a former slave; the Rev. Edmund Turney, founder and head of the National Theological Institute, a Baptist institution that educated freedmen for the ministry; and the Rev. William Jefferson White, an African American Baptist minister and cabinetmaker.

2

Chapter 1: The Founding Fathers and Early Presidents Era (1867-1906)

Richard Coulter was born a slave in Augusta and later fled to Washington, DC, to gain his freedom. Following the Civil War, Coulter received his formal education from the National Theological Institute (later merged with the American Baptist Home Society) in Washington, DC. After completing his educational training, Coulter successfully appealed to Rev. Turney to organize a new affiliate school of the National Theological Institute for former slaves in Augusta. With a letter of authorization from Rev. Turney, Coulter returned to Augusta in 1866 with admirable intentions to start a new school. However, feeling unable to organize the school, Coulter sought the aid of Rev. William Jefferson White, an established African American minister and cabinetmaker, who accepted the responsibility to start a branch of the Washington based Institute in Augusta. Coulter then wrote Rev. Turney, informing him what he had done. With authorization transferred to him, Rev. White secured a location for the school and recruited students. On February 14, 1867, Rev. White organized the school, sent a list of 37 names to the National Theological Institute for enrollment, and requested a teacher for the new school, which was named Augusta Institute. Because of the important role played by Rev. William Jefferson White, he is considered the "founder" of Augusta Institute (later named Morehouse College).[22]

William Jefferson White, the founder of Morehouse College.
Undated photo courtesy of the Morehouse College Archives.

Chapter 1: The Founding Fathers and Early Presidents Era (1867-1906)

Augusta Institute conducted its first classes at night in the basement of Springfield Baptist Church, one of the oldest independent Black churches in the United States. The Institute provided basic education with a theological emphasis. Each school session began with prayer, which was followed by roll call, then instruction. The textbooks used were an arithmetic book, a spelling book, and a Bible.

The original enrollment of students included male adult ministers and teenaged licentiates who worked on farms or assumed menial jobs during the day and administered their churches on Sundays.[23] During its first year of existence, enrollment fluctuated between the 38 and 60 students that came from the Augusta area. Most students were barely literate, but realizing the empowering benefits of education, they were eager to learn. They took short-term courses for a week or month at a time to improve their ability to serve as pastors and ministers of the Black churches of Augusta.

The early days of Augusta Institute were fairly unstable. Teachers were transient, and resources were scarce. Yet, two distinctive student traits emerged to create the Morehouse Mystique: a zeal for learning and a respect for teachers.

One of the most widely circulated newspapers in the United States in the 1860s, *Harper's Weekly*, reported that the person in charge of the school was a white man named Mr. Price (no first name mentioned). Instruction was reported to have been conducted by Miss Burt (no first name mentioned) and Miss Julia Sherman, both white missionaries from Brooklyn, New York, who volunteered their teaching services. Miss Sherman wrote a personal account of her experiences in *Harper's Weekly*:

"I had taught night school before, but never just this kind of school. Here were about forty ministers, of different ages, from the white-headed father...to the young licentiate, every one with a book in his hand and eager to study. They greeted us warmly, and when I said I hoped they would not have any objection to being taught by ladies temporarily they replied unanimously that they should consider it an honor."[24]

The Institute obtained a permanent school site in downtown Augusta on April 21, 1870. The first president of the Institute, Dr. Joseph Robert, served for 12 years, beginning on August 1, 1871, until his death on March 5, 1884. Dr. Robert, a white man of grand intellectual and moral stature, received his bachelor's degree from Brown University in 1828, did graduate work at Yale University, and obtained his medical degree from the University of South Carolina in 1831. He was both a physician and an ordained minister who served as pastor of several Baptist churches. Though born and raised in the South, Dr. Robert moved to the North before the Civil War because he did not wish to raise his children where slavery existed.

During his tenure as president, Dr. Robert almost single-handedly operated the school in the racially and politically hostile atmosphere of Augusta, where most white citizens opposed the education of African Americans. Moreover, the newly emancipated citizens of Augusta were denied the right to vote until March 23, 1873.[25] Without so much as one assistant for several years, Dr. Robert delivered lectures to students twice a week on Biblical and scientific

2)

subjects, evaluated student recitations for five hours a day, and raised funds from local Black Baptist churches, Northern white philanthropists, and the American Home Missionary Society to cover operational costs.

During Dr. Roberts' presidency, an average of 52 students was enrolled at any given time.[26] The early students of Augusta Institute were mostly adults and a few teenagers who came from towns and cities in Georgia, including Augusta, Atlanta, Brunswick, Elberton, and Herndon. Some students came from neighboring states, including South Carolina (Allendale), Alabama (Birmingham), and Florida (Tallahassee). The school administration valued the principles of hard work and self-cultivation and encouraged students to strive for racial uplift through religious evangelism.

Students were encouraged to supplement their studies by helping others and pursuing work related opportunities that developed their leadership skills. Some students served as Sunday school teachers, or they delivered occasional sermons at Augusta's Black churches. With their theological training, students developed a reputation for outstanding oratory. Upon returning to campus, the students had to give accounts of their community oriented missionary work at weekly meetings before their peers. Students also presided over weekly Wednesday night prayer services held on school grounds. These community and campus activities gave students the opportunity to improve their extemporaneous speaking abilities and to familiarize themselves with the methods of procedure in deliberative assemblies.

Dr. Robert's diligent efforts to establish this newly formed institution were not futile. By the end of the first decade of Augusta Institute's existence, its reputation had spread. Of the 245 students enrolled through 1878, 150 were ministerial

7

students[27] who went on to serve in churches throughout Georgia. Two students became missionaries in Africa, and two others were hired as missionaries by the Georgia Baptist Missionary Board and the American Baptist Home Missionary Society. One student, Augustus Johnson, became the first African American in Georgia to receive a public school license to build a school for African American children.[28]

The Early Leadership Mission

In 1879, several pivotal events occurred that deeply impacted the institution's future leadership mission. First, the school moved from Augusta to Atlanta, the state capital and one of the most populated cities in the Southeast. The physical relocation had both an immediate and long-term impact on Augusta's ability to actualize its leadership mission. More qualified faculty members were recruited, and more students were enrolled from the larger geographical area.

The move to the state capital was significant. Atlanta was becoming an intellectual hub of African American political and social thought in the South during the late 19th and early 20th centuries. Several other Black colleges and universities emerged in the city, which today, along with Morehouse College, form the Atlanta University Center. Prominent African American educators like Booker T. Washington, the head of the Tuskegee Normal and Industrial School (Tuskegee, Alabama), frequented the city. Washington delivered his famous "Atlanta Compromise" speech there in 1895.

Dr. William Edward Burghardt DuBois, author of the *Souls of Black Folk* (1903) and many other scholarly publications on the social conditions of African American

people, was a faculty member at Atlanta University (1897–
1910 and 1934–1944). With Augusta Institute now located in
Atlanta, an important hub of African American political,
social, and intellectual activity, students were exposed to the
most contemporary and cutting edge political, social, and
educational ideas.

Faculty, like DuBois and other national
leaders in the arts, sciences, government, and business,
exposed students to social and intellectual perspectives
unknown in Augusta and the towns and hamlets of the South.
The rigors of critical thinking and analysis, central to the
Morehouse Mystique, were further developed and expanded
in the Atlanta environment.

An ideological expansion of the school's mission
evolved from the singular focus of training ministers to include
the training of teachers, as reflected in the 1879 charter: "The
objects of the said corporation are to promote education among
the colored people of the South, especially by the training of
preachers and teachers of the colored race."[29]

Atlanta Baptist Seminary

In 1879, Augusta Institute underwent the second of
four name changes. It was renamed Atlanta Baptist Seminary
and adopted the motto *Et Facta Est Lux* ("And there was
light"), which signified the mission to illuminate the lives of
students. In 1885, the seminary moved from a temporary
location at Hunter and Elliot Streets, one block west of the
railroad terminal in downtown Atlanta, to its current setting
in West End, which, interestingly, had been a Confederate
battleground during the Civil War.

The second president, Dr. Samuel Graves, served from
1885 to 1890. Dr. Graves was described as "a man of singular

beauty and dignity of character, adding to sterling manliness, fervent piety, a tender sympathy for the needs of others, and a fine appreciation of the beautiful in art and literature."[30] He was a graduate of Colgate University, a former teacher of Greek at Kalamazoo College, and a former pastor of several northern churches. As president, Graves successfully expanded the campus and erected an administration building that today bears his name. During the cornerstone laying ceremony, the purpose of the newly erected Graves Hall was stated as "...the improvement of humanity, the instruction and enlightenment of a neglected people, and the acquisition of the moral and intellectual qualities which fit men for ...the respect and confidence of mankind."[31]

From the 1880s to the 1890s, the seminary enrolled both academically talented boys and adult men who had only an elementary education. Their teachers, high-minded young whites, were classically trained at colleges in the North. Despite the inherent challenges of teaching students with a wide range of academic preparation and abilities, the seminary offered a rigorously taught liberal arts curriculum. Students were expected to demonstrate superior moral and intellectual behaviors. They studied subjects such as Latin, Greek, chemistry, geology, logic, astronomy, and political economy over a four-year period, which prepared them for employment opportunities that were available to them after graduation.

Teaching a liberal arts curriculum to African American males in the late 19th century, however, had many critics. They countered that education should have a more practical, vocational focus. Dr. George Sale, a Canadian who served as the school's third president from 1890 to 1906, defended the academic focus, stating, "We aim not only at intellectual and spiritual culture, but also a social culture and the formation

10

of right domestic habits in our students."[32] And to his critics,
Dr. Sale further responded, "...if these studies have value for
white students, why should they not have the same value for
Negroes?"[33]
Despite the criticism, students were eager to learn,
and the single-sex composition of the student body facilitated
a spirit of brotherhood. Morehouse historian Benjamin
Brawley wrote:

> "The students were a heterogeneous lot. The
> average age was still high, but occasionally
> side by side with the man of 25 or 30 sat a boy
> of 14 who had better early advantages. No
> difference of age, however, disturbed the
> brotherly feeling that existed. All were poor
> boys, working for eight cents an hour... to help
> pay the expenses of board. The rough sturdy
> Christian fellowship rang through all, and
> made them inseparably one."[34]

Atlanta Baptist College

Thirty years after the school's founding, Atlanta
Baptist Seminary was granted "full college powers" in 1897
and was renamed Atlanta Baptist College.[35] Prior to this time,
students had only received theological certificates and high
school diplomas. With the new college status, the curriculum
included Latin, New Testament Greek, botany, algebra, and
geometry. The first class of students (Henry Bleach, John
Hubert, and Major Reddick) graduated with a bachelor's
degree in 1897. Bleach and Reddick became principals of
schools for African American youth within the state of

Georgia.[36] John Hubert obtained his master's degree from the University of Chicago, and he returned to Atlanta Baptist to head the science department. With the graduation of these men came the first tangible evidence that the leadership mission of the college was being fulfilled.

Toward the end of Dr. George Sale's 16-year presidency, an *espirit de corps*, characterized by a strong camaraderie, enthusiasm, devotion, and loyalty among students, began to manifest at the school.[37] Activities from football to debate were organized for students. Upperclassmen competed for the "Best Man of Affairs" prize, which was awarded to the senior who best exemplified the highest qualities of leadership, service, and academic excellence. Best Man of Affairs was the most coveted of awards for it defined in a single student the mystique of manhood that is the mission and purpose of the college. In 1908, the name of the prize was changed to honor a distinguished alumnus, J.J. Starks. The J.J. Starks Best Man of Affairs prize was awarded until the 1979–1980 academic year.

Dr. Sale inaugurated a policy of appointing graduates as full fledged faculty members. Alumni John Hubert, Benjamin Brawley, and C.H. Wardlaw were appointed. Several other promising African Americans who were educated in northern white colleges joined the ranks of the faculty as well, including John Hope and Samuel Archer, both of whom would serve as future presidents. These educators were the first in a long line of dedicated African American faculty who served the college throughout the 20th century. In 1906, Dr. Sale ended his tenure as president by giving a final emphatic charge to graduating students in his commencement address: "Boys, be men!"

Chapter 1: The Founding Fathers and Early Presidents Era (1867-1906)

The Early Presidential Legacy

The first three presidents of Morehouse College were white men, members of the ministry who possessed strong academic credentials. Their dedication, courage, and vision sustained the school in the face of racial hostility from its beginnings in the basement of Springfield Baptist Church in Augusta to its growth as a full-fledged college in Atlanta. The Morehouse Mystique materialized as each of these presidents embraced a strong religious conviction and planted the seeds of religious piety, brotherhood, hard work, and service to humanity into the institutional culture. Along with classroom instruction, Chapel, Bible study, debate, and athletics reinforced these institutional values among students.

Despite the many obstacles young African American students faced, they were transformed into leaders who would go on to provide a lifetime of service within their religious and educational communities. Dr. Henry Lyman Morehouse, who was the corresponding secretary of the American Baptist Home Mission Society, a primary funding and sponsoring agency for many Southern Black colleges, described the transformative effect:

> "In my years of service, I have seen the coarse boy become the talented preacher, the cultured professor, and the wise leader of thousands, and from long and wide acquaintances and observation I am prepared to say that the investment has paid hundredfold."[38]

The Morehouse Mystique

Rev. Henry L. Morehouse, photo caption from 1910 Hartshorn, W. N., & Penniman, G. W. (1910). *An era of progress and promise, 1863–1910: the religious, moral, and educational development of the American Negro since his emancipation.* Boston: Priscilla Publishing.

On June 7, 1913, Atlanta Baptist College was renamed Morehouse College in honor of Henry L. Morehouse, the long time friend and benefactor of the college.

Chapter 2: The John Hope Era
(1906–1940)

"We must develop men who can move among men in all
the walks of life, know their difficulties and
minister to their necessities...."[39]

Dr. John Hope
Morehouse College President

A new era of unprecedented growth, stability, and
national eminence emerged for Morehouse College on June
1, 1906, when Dr. John Hope assumed the presidency. At the
age of 37, Hope became the first African American president
of Morehouse College and one of the first African Americans
to lead a Black college in the United States.

Hope was born in Augusta, Georgia, in 1868. As a
child, he was mentored by Augusta Institute founder William
Jefferson White. Hope received his bachelor's degree from
Brown University, where he was elected to the Phi Beta Kappa
Honor Society. He later received an honorary master's degree
from Brown University and was granted honorary doctorates
by five universities.

During his 25-year presidency from 1906 to 1931, Dr.
Hope increased the college's annual enrollment from 21 to
359, enlarged the annual teaching budget from $7,000 to
$50,000, doubled the number of campus buildings, attracted
noted African American scholars to the faculty, and mentored
several students who ascended to national prominence in the
educational and political arenas. By the time of his death in
1936, the preeminent educator had created the college's
reputation as a "builder of men."[40]

The Morehouse Mystique

President John Hope, photo courtesy of the
Morehouse College Office of Communications

Dr. Hope's ascension to the presidency of Morehouse College reflected a shift from white to African American administrative control during a time of extreme racial hostility and oppression in the South. In the summer of 1906, just before Hope assumed the presidency of Morehouse, Atlanta was embroiled in one of the worse race riots in the nation's history. Many African American adults and some children were savagely beaten or shot to death by a white mob. The state of Georgia was a hotbed of racial hostility. The Ku Klux Klan was based in Stone Mountain, just east of Atlanta, and lynching by white mobs was a frequent occurrence in many rural communities throughout the state. Caricatures depicting racial stereotypes in mainstream newspapers in the South and throughout the nation frequently denigrated all African Americans, particularly males, as subhuman, lawless, lazy, and cowardly because they were considered threats to traditional American society.

Rare Periodicals and Newspapers Collection, *Le Petit Parisien* Newspaper, October 14, 1906, Atlanta Race Riot. Courtesy of the Auburn Avenue Research Library on African Culture & History.

The Hope Vision

Against this backdrop, Hope's appointment as president was a symbol of racial pride for Morehouse students and faculty as well as African Americans in Atlanta and throughout the South. Hope transformed Morehouse College into a powerful instrument of racial uplift through the rigorous leadership and intellectual training of African American males. Hope's greatest contribution as president was his insistence that education be used by students as a means of racial uplift and racial solidarity among African Americans.

This vision of leadership was emphasized by Dr. Hope at the Morehouse College 50th Founders' Day anniversary in February 1917:

> "... the avowed and unshaken purpose of Morehouse College (is) leadership. Whether with the spelling book or a course in chemistry, whether in a prayer meeting or in the abandon of a football game, the purpose is the making of leaders, and these leaders must be Christian. With the half-century's unfolding of this college's purpose it is found constantly and consistently this—training for Christian leadership."[41]

The Influence of Dr. William Edward Burghardt DuBois

During his tenure at Morehouse as a faculty member and later as president, Dr. Hope became a close friend, ally, and associate of W.E.B. DuBois. As the first African American to obtain a Ph.D. from Harvard University, DuBois was one of the most distinguished educators of the 20th century. DuBois promulgated the ideology that the improvement of the plight of Black people rested with the Talented Tenth, the brightest minds of the African American race. In 1903 he wrote:

"The Negro race, like all races, is going to be saved by its exceptional men. The problem of education, then, among Negroes must first of all deal with the Talented Tenth; it is the problem of developing the Best of this race that they may guide the Mass away from the contamination and death of the Worst, in their own and other races."[42]

Dr. W.E.B. DuBois in 1918

Hope wholeheartedly embraced DuBois' ideology, believing that "people who were advantaged ought to help the people who were less advantaged."[43] In 1905, Hope, DuBois, and other African American progressives founded the Niagara Movement, an unashamedly radical Black organization that renounced the social accommodation policies set forth by Booker T. Washington in his "Atlanta Compromise" speech of 1895. A foe of segregation, Hope was the only Black college president to attend this founding meeting. He was also present at the founding of the National Association for the Advancement of Colored People (NAACP) in 1909.

Hope's passion for political activism as a means of racial uplift and equality was reflected in the educational arena. His belief in the intellectual and ethical development of leaders inspired his efforts to solidify the academic program at Morehouse, which quickly began to manifest results. For example, in 1910, DuBois rated Morehouse College as one of the top quality Black colleges in America, identifying it as a "First-Grade Colored College."[44]

Academic Life

As president, Hope publicly denounced the educational philosophy of Booker T. Washington. He demonstrated great courage by defying the popular trend of promoting industrial and vocational training exclusively for African Americans. Instead, Hope boldly championed a liberal arts education by expanding the Morehouse College curriculum to include the sciences. In 1921, under his visionary leadership, Morehouse became the first Black college in the United States to designate a permanent building exclusively for the teaching of the sciences. It was originally named Science Hall.[45] Science Hall (later renamed Hope Hall in honor of John Hope) housed biology, chemistry, and physics classrooms, faculty offices, laboratories, and a greenhouse.

That same year, Morehouse College accepted the first group of students who sought the Bachelor of Science degree. Four years later (1925), five students graduated with a

Bachelor of Science degree, and four of the five ultimately became medical doctors.[46] These graduates marked a turning point and laid a strong foundation for the college's reputation as a producer of more African American Ph.D.'s in the sciences than any other American college.[47]

In addition to an emphasis on the sciences, in the 1920s and 1930s, Morehouse offered a variety of theoretical and practical courses in other disciplines that were designed to encourage leadership in a number of professions. For example, the Department of Economics and Business offered courses in economics, accounting, and marketing. The Department of Education offered courses in methods and principles of teaching in elementary and secondary schools, the history of education, and psychology. The departments of chemistry, physics, biology, and geology offered courses in their respective disciplines as well.

President John Hope, front center, with Morehouse College
faculty and staff.
Undated photo courtesy of Morehouse College Archives.

The Morehouse Mystique

During the Hope era, the faculty included a small cadre of dedicated African American men and women, including Burrell T. Harvey, Walter Chivers (class of 1919), Samuel Archer, Claude Dansby (class of 1922), Charles Hubert, Kemper Harrell, Nathaniel P. Tillman (class of 1920), and E. Franklin Frazier, all of whom received graduate training at some of the best universities opened to African Americans at the time. Hope personally recruited his faculty, and they embraced his educational philosophy of racial uplift.

Teachers were paid a small salary of $1,200–1,800 a year, but they were uncommonly dedicated and instilled in their students an appreciation for character, accuracy, and enthusiasm.[48] Faculty and staff were renowned for promoting a climate of self-discipline and high expectations among students. Of the teachers who came to Morehouse during the Hope era was Benjamin Mays, a mathematics teacher and debate coach who would later serve as president from 1940 to 1967. Reflecting upon the rigorous demands of the program Mays stated: "Morehouse students learned from faculty that their reach should exceed their grasp and never accept that the ceiling was the limit of their striving (but) rather the sky was his goal…."[49]

Student Life

Though not a minister, Dr. Hope was a deeply religious man who prayed at the beginning of his chapel talks to students. The Morehouse College of his day reflected his religious character, as evidenced in the school's catalog description:

Chapter 2: The John Hope Era
(1906-1940)

"...a Christian School for the education of
Young Negro Men, operated by the American
Baptist Home Missionary Society of Northern
States—strong faculty, fine equipment, grades,
academy, college, (and) divinity school."[50]

Students were mostly first generation college students
from cities like Atlanta, Nashville, and Birmingham, or rural
communities like Lake View, Arkansas, Green Cove Springs,
Florida, and LaGrange, Georgia. They were poor; some were
able to enroll only because of scholarships and tuition
assistance from the American Baptist Home Missionary
Society. The intimate campus setting facilitated close contact
among students, administrators, and faculty and allowed Hope
and the faculty to indoctrinate students with religious values.
Students were expected to embody characteristics of "self-
mastery, symmetrical character, and high ideals and
purposes."[51]

Hope was a strong-willed disciplinarian who
demanded that students abide by a strict code of conduct.
Dancing, fraternizing with females without an adult
chaperone, and smoking were not permitted on campus. One
student was not allowed to enter the college because he
allegedly "kissed a girl" while driving back to the school from
a football game in Knoxville, Tennessee,[52] and another student
was suspended for playing cards in his dorm room. A group
of students was also chastised because they were caught
holding hands with students from Spelman College, the
neighboring female school adjacent to Morehouse.[53]

Hope was also a very caring man who was greatly
admired and considered by students as "genteel, scholarly,
(and) decorous."[54] Hope visibly wore his Phi Beta Kappa key
from a chain on his vest everyday, a reminder to impressionable

students of the importance of academic excellence. In addition to his presidential duties, Hope served as the college treasurer and a professor of logic, psychology, and ethics. These multiple roles allowed Hope to establish and cultivate a close connection with students and parents and to positively impact the character development of students.

During the Hope era, African American men were subjected to constant physical and verbal assaults. Their "manhood was denied on all levels by white society" and occurrences of "lynchings, burnings, and unspeakable cruelties" were everyday reminders that their "lives were of little value."[55] Yet, Hope discreetly strengthened the "faltering egos" of students by respectfully addressing them as "men of Morehouse," "young gentleman," or "mister," in stark contrast to whites who generally referred to any African American man, regardless of age or social standing, as "boy," "uncle," "nigger," or his first name.[56]

The 1923 college yearbook described Hope as "...a profound Christian scholar, who sees and makes others see...and who...as president has kept faith with the ideals and aims of Morehouse College...."[57] Hope's interest in his students extended beyond graduation. He helped students enroll in prestigious graduate schools, counseled them in their first jobs, and reminded them of their social responsibility to uplift the Black community. In a letter to a 1923 graduate, Hope advised, "Keep your eyes open and not allow a desire for a dollar or for popularity to make you do things that are absolutely against our progress in the long run..."[58] This counsel was consistent with his belief and commitment to the continued development of each Morehouse Man and the uplift of the African American community.

Chapter 2: The John Hope Era
(1906-1940)

Daily Chapel

The most prominent co-curricular activity during the Hope era was Chapel. As a Christian college, Morehouse provided both morning and evening chapel services nearly every day of the week; attendance at these services was mandatory for all students. Chapel was held in the intimate setting of Sale Hall, a three story building built in 1910 and named after former Morehouse president George Sale. The principle aim of Chapel was the spiritual, moral, and intellectual leadership development of students and was considered by some students to be the "greatest single course of instruction" at Morehouse.[59]

Morehouse students attending Chapel.
Undated photo courtesy of the Morehouse College Archives

To facilitate the spiritual and moral development of students, the daily morning Chapel, which began at 9:30 a.m., consisted of a one-hour service of prayer and readings from scripture and culminated in a sermon, speech, or lecture delivered by Hope, a member of the faculty, a prominent preacher, or outside experts in certain fields. Chapel on Tuesday was reserved for Hope's "family talk" sessions in which he discussed students' social responsibility towards the Black community. On the first Sunday of each month (First Sunday Chapel), a minister from Atlanta would address the college community.

Night Chapel was a leadership activity used for student self-governance and self-development. Night Chapel was held after dinner every night of the week except Friday. The President of the Senior Class appointed a student to preside over these services. One of the activities of night Chapel was public speaking. Each student was required to deliver an original oration for each of his four undergraduate years. This activity was designed to improve students' leadership and public speaking abilities, "an unmistakable mark of the Morehouse training."[60]

During the morning chapel services, attendance was monitored and absences were not tolerated. Students sat in assigned seats according to a hierarchal seating arrangement: seniors sat in the front rows, juniors in the middle rows, sophomores in the rear, and freshmen in the balcony.

The greatest benefit of Chapel was that it provided a common experience for students to become indoctrinated in the moral and intellectual values and ideals espoused by the college. Also, Morehouse students were kept informed about issues of importance on local, regional, national, and international levels. Prominent African Americans and Morehouse alumni were often guest lecturers. Some of the chapel topics included "The Romance of Astronomy," "The Negro Family," "The World of Negro Business," and "The Negro in Politics."[61]

Chapter 2: The John Hope Era
(1906-1940)

Student Activities

Morehouse College viewed student activities as supportive of and harmonious with the overall educational program. Students were encouraged to get involved in campus activities as a way to "secure an understanding, an appreciation, a comprehensive view of the whole of life, and a grasp of the magnitude of man's possibilities within himself."[62] The administration embraced a democratic tradition in which students and faculty participated jointly on all college committees and decided on issues and programs that affected the life of the college family.

In 1929, the foundation for a student government association was established and was called the "Student Body." Students voted to pay a fee of $12 to support athletics and other campus activities.[63] Student activities included the debate team, the Glee Club, athletics, the Young Men's Christian Association, student government, and fraternities. Students became culturally sophisticated through their exposure to performances by the college orchestra and the drama club's Shakespearean plays.

The most prominent activities involved the debate team and the Glee Club. Debate was a formal intercollegiate activity at Morehouse that dated back to 1906 when the college competed against Talladega College, a historically Black college in Alabama. Debating was considered an intellectual activity as well as a means of developing the art of speech. Students considered membership on the debate team as prestigious, and the selection process was competitive. The debate team consisted of four varsity men and two alternates. Morehouse was part of the larger "Triangular Debating League," which was formed in 1911 along with two other historically Black colleges, Talladega College and Knoxville

College. The Morehouse debate team also competed against white schools like the University of Vermont and Bucknell University and engaged in international competition against Cambridge University and Oxford University.[5]

Debate Team, *The Torch*, 1923, Samuel Howard Archer Collection, Atlanta-Fulton Public Library System, Auburn Avenue Research Library of History and Culture.

Chapter 2: The John Hope Era
(1906-1940)

The Glee Club, which traces its origins to 1911, is considered the "official singing organization of Morehouse" and has a vibrant, long-standing tradition.[65] The founder of the Glee Club, Professor Kemper Harrell, a graduate of the Chicago Musical College, had continued his studies in Berlin before joining the Morehouse faculty. Under his directorship, the Glee Club became a major student organization and served as the official choir of the college.

While its purpose was to teach Morehouse students to sing and play musical instruments, the Glee Club played an important role in student leadership development. Glee Club members learned presentation skills, discipline, and showmanship. Over the years, the Glee Club has made many notable appearances, including command performances before President Franklin D. Roosevelt at his presidential retreat in Warm Springs, Georgia, the funeral of Dr. Martin Luther King, Jr., the inauguration ceremony of President Jimmy Carter, and the welcoming ceremony for His Imperial Majesty Emperor Haile Selassie of Ethiopia when he visited the United States.[66] Along with campus activities, Morehouse students were encouraged to participate in the local Black communities of Atlanta. Many Morehouse students were the sons of ministers, and nearly every student taught a Sunday school class in one of the area's churches. Morehouse students provided leadership in these churches and served as inspirational role models to youth and adults.

Espirit de Corps

The *espirit de corps* that was embraced by students in the 1890's grew stronger during the Hope era. Competition among students was intense but healthy, as students often referred to each other as "brother." The school motto, "One for all and all for one," exemplified a spirit of oneness and brotherhood throughout the campus. Seniors were permitted to sit together in the campus dining room at the "senior tables" where they engaged in word games to increase their vocabulary.[67] Others competed to read every book in the college library.

In 1929, Morehouse senior J. Orville B. Moseley composed "Dear Old Morehouse," a song that embodied the Morehouse spirit and love for his alma mater. Moseley presented the words of the song to the student body; students received it with much joy and enthusiasm. It thereafter was adopted as the College Hymn and is sung at each official college function today:

Dear Old Morehouse

Dear old Morehouse, dear old Morehouse,
We have pledged our lives to thee;
And we'll ever, yea forever
Give ourselves in loyalty.
True forever, true forever,
To old Morehouse may we be;
So to bind each son the other
Into ties more brotherly.
Holy Spirit, Holy Spirit,
Make us steadfast, honest, true,
To old Morehouse, and her ideals,
And in all things that we do.

Chapter 2: The John Hope Era
(1906-1940)

Considered a sacred and somber hymn by Morehouse students and alumni, all participants rise and link arms right over left while singing. During the first two verses of the last stanza, heads are bowed reverently. As the last two verses of the last stanza are sung, heads are raised, and the song ends on an exuberantly joyful note. The lyrics speak to the loyalty that students have for "Dear Old Morehouse," the brotherhood that students and alumni share with each other, the strong character traits Morehouse Men should strive to embody, and the recognition of the Supreme Being.

The Emergence of the First Nationally Renowned Leaders

During the Hope era, the sum total of all curricular and extracurricular activities was leadership development, and this sense of mission profoundly affected the students.[68] The 1923 *Torch* Yearbook reads, "...the college emphasizes clean Christian manhood, which redirects the misguided lives of men and creates a pressing demand for Morehouse men as social service workers."[69] Students took their responsibility to use their knowledge and training to uplift the Black community seriously. Beginning in 1911, several graduates embraced this call to service and began to rise to national prominence during the 1930s and 1940s. Many of these individuals were early pioneers of the civil rights movement.

The first of the Morehouse graduates to rise to national prominence was Rev. Mordecai Wyatt Johnson from Paris, Tennessee. Johnson enrolled at Morehouse in 1905. While a student, Johnson was a star athlete in three sports (he was quarterback of the football team) and a member of the debate team and Glee Club. Following his graduation with honors in

1911, Johnson was offered a faculty position to teach English and economics at Morehouse; he served a year as acting dean. Afterwards, Johnson earned additional degrees from the University of Chicago and the Rochester Theological Institute.

In 1917, Johnson became pastor of the First Baptist Church of Charleston, West Virginia, and served for nine years. Johnson later obtained his Master's of Divinity at Harvard University in 1922. While at Harvard, his oratorical ability won him such critical acclaim that he was selected to deliver the commencement address. Considered a bold, defiant African American man with a persuasive oratorical style, Johnson was quoted as saying, "When a man speaks the truth, supported by ethical and moral living, girded with a deep spirituality, nothing can stop him, except illness and death."[70] In 1926, at the age of 36, Johnson became the first African American president of Howard University. While leading in that post until 1960, Howard became one of the premier institutions in America. Throughout his years as Howard's president, Mordecai Johnson frequently returned to Morehouse College. He spoke at Dr. John Hope's funeral, occasionally served as a chapel speaker, served as the 1949 commencement speaker, and was a confidante of Dr. Benjamin Mays. He also had a profound influence on fellow Morehouse graduates, particularly on Dr. Martin Luther King's commitment to nonviolence resistance, which will be explained in greater detail in the chapter on Dr. King.

The second distinguished Morehouse graduate was Dr. Howard Thurman, an internationally renowned theologian who served as the dean of Rankin Chapel (Howard University) and Marsh Chapel (Boston University). Thurman was born in Daytona, Florida, and became the first African American child from his hometown to earn a high school diploma.[71] In the spring of his senior year (1919), Thurman met Morehouse alumnus and First Baptist pastor Rev. Johnson while attending a Christian Student Leadership Conference. Johnson encouraged Thurman to "finish high school, go to college, and go on to graduate school." Impressed by Johnson, an "articulate, well-dressed, well-educated young minister," Thurman decided that Morehouse should be his "college of choice."[72] Thurman entered Morehouse as a freshman in 1919. While at Morehouse, Thurman was active on the debate team, editor of the yearbook, and graduated as class valedictorian in 1923. Thurman was described by his peers as "our most brilliant classmate" and "the personification of the Morehouse Ideal—a genuine Christian."[73] He was mentored by President John Hope and Professor E. Franklin Frazier, the latter Thurman described as an "example of scholarship."[74]

After graduating from Morehouse, Thurman attended Rochester Theological Seminary and was ordained a Baptist minister in 1925. He returned to Morehouse in 1929 to teach religion before being named by his mentor, Rev. Johnson, the first dean of Rankin Chapel at Howard University. He was later appointed as the first African American dean at Marsh Chapel at Boston University.

Throughout his professional life, Thurman traveled broadly, heading Christian missions and meeting with world figures like Mahatma Gandhi in 1936. When Thurman asked Gandhi what message he should take back to America, Gandhi said he regretted not having made nonviolence more visible worldwide and hoped an American Black man would succeed where he had failed. In 1943, Thurman founded the Fellowship Church for all People, the nation's first interracial, interfaith church, located in San Francisco.

Among the people whose lives were touched by
Thurman was Dr. Martin Luther King, Jr. King frequently
read from Thurman's book *Jesus and the Disinherited*
(published in 1949), which provided much of the philosophical
foundation for the modern nonviolent civil rights movement.
Like other prominent alumni, Dr. Howard Thurman frequently
returned to Morehouse to speak and interact with students. In
1950, he was the commencement speaker and was quoted as
saying the following about Morehouse's institutional culture:
"Over the heads of her students Morehouse holds a crown
that she challenges them to grow tall enough to wear," a
frequently referenced mantra to this day. Before his death in
1981, *Ebony* magazine called Thurman one of the 50 most
important figures in African American history, and in 1961,
Life magazine rated him among the 12 best preachers in the
nation.

The third renowned graduate was James Nabrit, Jr., a
leading civil rights lawyer of his generation who actively
participated in many of the seminal civil rights cases in the
1940s and 1950s. James Nabrit was born in Atlanta, Georgia,
and enrolled at Morehouse in 1919.

As a Morehouse student, Nabrit was active in campus
activities, including the football team, the YMCA, and debate
team. During his sophomore year, Nabrit received debate
coaching from none other than Dr. Benjamin E. Mays. One
of his teammates was Howard Thurman.

Nabrit was described by his Morehouse College peers
as "the perambulating epitome of efficiency."[75] He graduated
with honors in 1923, along with his friend and classmate
Howard Thurman. After attending Northwestern University
Law School, he joined Howard's law faculty in 1936. Two

years later, he taught the first formal civil rights law course to be offered at any law school in the United States.

Along with teaching, Nabrit handled a number of civil rights cases for the NAACP Legal Defense and Educational Fund, working closely with imminent civil rights attorneys such as Charles Hamilton Houston and Thurgood Marshall. Nabrit served as dean of the Howard University School of Law from 1958 to 1960 during the presidency of fellow Morehouse alumnus Rev. Mordecai Wyatt Johnson.

Nabrit was appointed Howard University's second African American president, a position he held from 1960 to 1965 and again from 1968 to 1969. The Morehouse legacy in the Howard University presidency is significant and decisive in the development of the civil rights movement, especially as it led to the March on Washington in 1963. In between these presidential tenures, Nabrit represented the United States as deputy ambassador to the United Nations in 1966.

The fourth student of national acclaim to graduate during the Hope era was Dr. Samuel Nabrit (class of 1925), the younger brother of James Nabrit. After the younger's graduation from Morehouse, President Hope hired him at the age of 20 to chair the Morehouse Biology Department. In 1932, Samuel Nabrit entered Brown University and received a Ph.D. in biological sciences, becoming the first African American man to receive a doctorate degree from Brown. He was a member of Dwight Eisenhower's National Science Board and in 1966 was appointed by President Lyndon B. Johnson as the first African American to serve on the Atomic Energy Commission. Samuel Nabrit served as president of Texas Southern University from 1955 to 1966, and in 1967, he became the first African American trustee at Brown University.

By 1927, ten Morehouse grads were serving as college presidents, leading such schools as Jackson State College, Benedict College, and Morris College. This impressive track record gave Morehouse College the reputation of "maker of college presidents."[76] By the 1930s, Morehouse College had produced graduates in a variety of professions; they included seven college deans and registrars, 40 college teachers, 21 school principals, 52 public and private school teachers, 128 ministers, 36 physicians and dentists, and seven lawyers.[77]

The Hope Legacy

Like his presidential predecessors, John Hope was a visionary leader. Toward the end of his presidency at Morehouse, he played an instrumental role in Atlanta University, Spelman College, and Morehouse College, forming a consortium known as the Atlanta University Center. The Center later expanded to include Clark College, Morris Brown College, and the Interdenominational Theological Center. Today these member colleges collectively enroll the most African American students seeking baccalaureate degrees than anywhere else in the United States.

From 1929 to 1931, Hope served as president of Atlanta University while simultaneously holding onto his post as president of Morehouse College. In 1929, Hope received the Harmon Award in Education for "distinguished service in furthering the education of the Negro race."[78] In 1931, John Hope resigned his presidency of Morehouse College and remained president of Atlanta University until his death in 1936.

Hope's greatest legacy was his influence on the climate of academic excellence at Morehouse. Under his leadership,

Chapter 2: The John Hope Era
(1906-1940)

Morehouse obtained membership in the Association of American Colleges, the American Association of Collegiate Registrars, The Association of Colleges for Negro Youth, and the National Association of Collegiate Deans and Registrars in Negro Schools. By 1933, the college had achieved a Class I rating by the American Medical Association, which was the premiere pre-medical rating body in America.[79] Morehouse also received a Class A rating by the Southern Association of Colleges and Secondary Schools and the American Medical Association, which affirmed that the credits and degrees conferred by the college would be accepted by graduate and medical schools.

Hope not only affected the campus culture of excellence, he placed his personal signature on students. As their "guiding mentor," the seeds of self worth and confidence, long dormant within African American men of his era, began to germinate and sprout.[80] Morehouse students developed a positive attitude about themselves, their sense of self grew, and they were identified as "Morehouse Men" or one of "John Hope's men."[81] Dr. Hope never let them forget that the purpose of their academic training and leadership skills was to uplift the Black community.

Toward the end of Hope's presidential tenure, Morehouse College was achieving phenomenal success in graduating African American men and preparing them for graduate programs and professional careers. For example, in 1936, 34 percent of Morehouse graduates entered graduate programs, 25 percent entered the teaching profession, and 41 percent entered other professions. By 1939, 39 percent went on to graduate school, 29 percent went into teaching, and 30 percent went into business, insurance, or government work.[82] The overwhelming majority of Morehouse College graduates seeking graduate studies or entering professional careers is a true testament of Hope's actualization of his vision for leadership development.

On February 20, 1936, John Hope died of pneumonia in Atlanta. He was revered and loved by the entire Morehouse College family. Samuel Archer, who succeeded Hope as president, stated in his eulogy that "he loved Morehouse only like a father loves his son."[83]

Though noted for his contributions to Morehouse College, Hope also had been a nationally acclaimed leader in the community. In recognition of his outstanding service in the academic arena as well as being a pioneer in race relations, Hope received numerous awards, including five honorary doctorate degrees. Hope posthumously received the prestigious NAACP Spingarn Medal, which recognized him as "one of the foremost (college) presidents in the United States, widely and favorably known throughout the educational world."[84] Hope was buried on the campus grounds of Atlanta University on February 23, 1936, bordering Morehouse College. As a tribute to Hope and his contributions to the college, a graveside service is held each year as part of Morehouse's commencement exercises.

Chapter 3: The Dr. Benjamin E. Mays Era (1940–1967)

"The Morehouse College graduate not only must be intellectually competent but he must be morally competent. A Morehouse Man must be known by the quality of his work, the quality of his life and the quality of his contribution to society. If such is not the aim of Morehouse College, it has no right to exist. The future of mankind depends upon such leadership."[85]

Dr. Benjamin E. Mays
President, Morehouse College

While Dr. John Hope laid the foundation for a culture of excellence at Morehouse College, the man who elevated the college to a cathedral of excellence was Dr. Benjamin Elijah Mays. Mays served as president of Morehouse from 1940 to 1967, the longest tenure of any Morehouse president to date. During the Mays reign, the United States endured major historical events that impacted Morehouse College, including World War II, the civil rights movement, the Brown vs. Topeka Board Supreme Court decision, and the eventual dismantling of Jim Crow segregation laws throughout the South. Under Mays' leadership, many graduates would rise as leaders of national and international acclaim.

Dr. Benjamin Mays was a prolific writer, wise theologian, outstanding orator, distinguished statesman, and astute scholar. He traveled worldwide and was an advisor to U.S. Presidents John F. Kennedy and Lyndon B. Johnson.

Mays came from humble beginnings. He was born in
1894 in a rural community near the town of Ninety-Six, South
Carolina, and attended high school in neighboring
Orangeburg, where he graduated as valedictorian of his senior
class. In 1920, Mays graduated from Bates College with a
bachelor's degree and Phi Beta Kappa honors.

In 1921, President John Hope hired Mays to teach
higher mathematics and psychology at Morehouse. Mays had
a reputation as a highly demanding, no-nonsense teacher. He
told students, "If you are one minute late to class, you cannot
come in."[86] Along with his teaching responsibilities, Mays
was the debate team coach, and he served as pastor of Shiloh
Baptist Church in Atlanta.

In 1924, Mays resigned his teaching post at Morehouse
to pursue graduate study at the University of Chicago, where
he received his Master of Arts Degree in 1925 and Ph.D. in
Ethics and Christian Theology from the Divinity School in
1935. From 1925 to 1940, Mays held a variety of
administrative positions, including serving as Student
Secretary of the YMCA and Dean of the School of Religion
at Howard University.

The Mays Vision

When Mays returned to Morehouse to become
president in 1940 at the age of 45, he inherited what he
described in his inauguration speech as "a great institution."
Yet, Mays pledged his all to make Morehouse an even greater
educational institution. At the Opening Chapel Service (his
first public address as Morehouse College president) on
September 18, 1940, Dr. Mays articulated his vision and

commitment to increase the "high regard" of Morehouse College in the eyes of the "thinkers of America":

> "When you come to Morehouse, you are coming to an institution that has achieved greatness primarily because of what its graduates have accomplished since the founding of the College in 1867.
>
> I stand here with fear and trembling because I know what a great responsibility it is to try to direct the thinking and to develop the character of young people.
>
> I do promise you...before God, that I will give to Morehouse College all that I have. I will give to this institution and to you the best of my mind, heart, and soul...." [87]

Mays was an imposing and inspirational figure who continued the tradition of his predecessors in stressing academic excellence, religious piety with a social conscience, and a commitment to racial advancement. Mays emphasized these principles in his speeches, writings, and daily interactions with Morehouse students and faculty. Faculty described him as a "master motivator" and alumni described him as a "militant, active, wise crusader for human rights (and) a gentleman and a scholar whose example serves to inspire those with whom he works and those whom he leads..."[88] Benjamin Mays was respected by his peers and revered by students. Dr. Mays was a larger than life African

American intellectual giant, a tremendous role model for students.
Dr. Louis Sullivan, an Atlanta native and Morehouse graduate (class of 1954), became president of the Morehouse School of Medicine (1975–1989 and 1993–2002) and was appointed in 1991 by President George H. Bush as Secretary of the U.S. Department of Health and Human Services. According to Sullivan, "Dr. Mays had the eloquence, plus the physical presence. He was not a very tall man…but he stood straight, had this imposing gray hair, piercing eyes, gentle smile and friendly, but for students, he was a formidable figure. He was our role model…."[89]

Another student influenced by Mays was Al Price (class of 1950), a Beaumont, Texas, native who entered Morehouse as a 16-year old in 1946. Price became one of the first pilots to work for a U.S. commercial airline and a Texas state representative. Reflecting on Mays, Price said, "Morehouse took me as a little green kid (and) …for the first time I saw a real African American scholar and orator and it was just mesmerizing."[90]

Academic Life

Dr. Mays cultivated a distinguished cadre of faculty and staff with impeccable academic credentials received from the few graduate schools that admitted African American students, including Harvard University, Columbia University, and New York University. Mays often boasted about the accomplished faculty that had been assembled under his presidential watch. He fervently believed that a quality faculty was the strength of an educational institution.

Chapter 3: The Dr. Benjamin E. Mays Era
(1940-1967)

In 1945, among a faculty, nine had earned doctorates, 14 had master's degrees, and one had a bachelor's degree. The faculty included such men and women as James Birnie (class of 1930), Brailsford Brazeal (class of 1927), Robert Brisbane, Hugh Gloster (class of 1931), Edward Jones (class of 1926), George Kelsey (class of 1934), Melvin Kennedy, Frederick Mapp (class of 1932), Henry McBay, Edward Buchannan Williams (class of 1928), and Mary Reddick.[91]

Mays constantly challenged his faculty to mentor and inspire students:

> "In our desperate struggle to build a better plant, get finer equipment, and secure high degreed teachers, we must also strive to develop students who have a zeal for learning and who seek knowledge as blind men seeks light; and teachers who not only teach, but teachers who inspire students to do their best."[92]

Mays also recruited many white teachers, men and women, from the South. He believed it was "good to bring together Southern white teachers and black students" as a means to bridge the racial gulf.[93]

During May's tenure, the academic curriculum consisted of courses in a variety of disciplines, including religion, philosophy, physical sciences, social sciences, humanities, and foreign languages. The mandatory core curriculum was designed to cultivate an appreciation across a broad spectrum of issues in the arts and sciences. Some courses, for example, those offered in the Department of Political Science, inspired students to challenge racial discrimination.

U.S. Federal Judge Horace T. Ward (class of 1949), a Morehouse graduate from LaGrange, Georgia, shares how one such course influenced his decision to enter the legal profession:

> "Among the courses that I took, one that most greatly effected my professional aspirations was a course on Constitutional Law, taught by Dr. Robert Brisbane during my senior year. Dr. Brisbane was a brilliant, proud African American man, who had recently obtained his doctorate from Harvard University. He taught us about lawsuit cases, such as the Lloyd Gaines case at the University of Missouri, which challenged and overturned school desegregation in the South. This course inspired me greatly and planted the idea in my mind that I should one day challenge the discriminatory practices of a white, Southern school, so that I could get my law school training."[94]

After his graduation from Morehouse, Ward obtained his Master's degree in Political Science at Atlanta University. In September 1950, Ward applied to the University of Georgia Law School, becoming the first African American to challenge the discriminatory practices of that university (with the help of the NAACP Legal Defense and Education Fund). For three years, Ward's case for admission was tied up in the court system. Although his effort was unsuccessful, his case helped lay the groundwork for desegregation.

Chapter 3: The Dr. Benjamin E. Mays Era
(1940-1967)

After completing his law school degree in 1959 at Northwestern University, Ward returned to Georgia and assisted attorneys Donald Hollowell and Constance Baker Motley in their efforts to desegregate the University of Georgia. On January 6, 1961, a judge ordered the university to admit two African American students: Hamilton E. Holmes and Charlayne A. Hunter, thus ending 175 years of segregation at the university.

Horace T. Ward (class of 1949), speaking at Paschal's Restaurant in Atlanta in the 1960's.
Photo courtesy of the Morehouse College Archives.

Dr. Mays raised scholarship funds from the philanthropic community so that he could recruit students of high academic caliber but who had limited financial resources. Memphis native Major Owens (class of 1956) received a scholarship from the Ford Foundation. He went on to serve in the U.S. Congress from 1983 to 2007 (11th District, Brooklyn, New York). Owens described the academic climate among his peers:

> "For the first time I was in an atmosphere with folks with IQ's higher than mine and seemed to be able to grasp what was going on faster than I did. So, the experience of being in that kind of group, being close to youngsters with that kind of ability, who were striving and ambitious, that was a great experience."[95]

By recruiting excellent faculty and talented students, Mays fostered an academically competitive atmosphere on campus. Students who displayed academic excellence were rewarded. Each semester, students who earned a 3.0 grade point average were recognized at an Honors Day ceremony. The names of top achieving students were printed on the Honors Day program.

Student Life

Throughout Mays' administration, student enrollment was relatively low. World War II and the draft called young men into active duty. As a result, in 1944, student enrollment dropped to 345 students. However, by 1946, enrollment grew to 826 and to 1,037 by 1967, the end of Mays' presidency.

Chapter 3: The Dr. Benjamin E. Mays Era
(1940-1967)

In the early years of Mays' presidency, Morehouse attracted students from 20 different states, mostly Georgia, Alabama, and Florida.[96] Promising students of high intellect and demonstrated abilities converged at Morehouse at a time when scholarships were becoming more widely available. Leroy Johnson (class of 1949) entered Morehouse in 1945. In 1962, he was elected as the first African American senator to serve in the Georgia State Legislature since Reconstruction. According to Johnson, the seeds of responsibility and service were planted in the hearts and minds of students:

> "While a student, I was privileged to develop friendships with several other Morehouse students, who later in life would become national and local leaders. These included classmates such as U.S. Federal Judge Horace Ward, Civil Rights activist Dr. C. Clayton Powell, and Ebony Magazine editor, Lerone Bennett. I was also an associate of Dr. Martin L. King, Jr., who was a member of the class of 1948. At the time, we were all just ordinary students, but we heard the same 'call of service' that was a central message of Morehouse and became inspired to make a difference."[97]

The small student enrollment made it easy for Dr. Mays to maintain a good rapport with students. He personally knew many students and alumni by first name. The presidential residence was located on the Morehouse campus, and Dr.

Mays and his wife, Sadie, frequently hosted students in their home, using these occasions to impart table manners and other social etiquette skills to students.

Morehouse students dining in the Mays' home with Dr. and Mrs. Mays.
Photo courtesy of the Morehouse College Archives.

Under Dr. Mays, the number of extracurricular activities grew. In addition to student government, fraternities, the Glee Club, Orchestra, and the debate team, the *Maroon Tiger* student newspaper and the Torch yearbook were added. These activities were important in developing the whole man—mind, body, and soul. Dr. Mays expected excellence from students not only in academics but in all campus activities, including athletics. For example, Mays wrote the following admonishment in the *Morehouse Alumnus* magazine:

> "Morehouse men ought to play better football than they play.... We do mind when Morehouse loses seven games out of eight. We do mind our getting beat when it is clear that the men have not been properly disciplined and when it is clear that the men are not physically fit and mentally alert on the field. I am not fussing because we get beat. I am fussing because we do not play to our capacity...."[98]

Daily Chapel

The daily Chapel tradition that was institutionalized during the Hope administration continued during Mays' presidential tenure. Like Hope, Mays used Chapel as a way to influence and expose students to a plethora of ideas and perspectives. Dr. Mays upheld Dr. Hope's tradition of giving his own "family talk" sessions on Tuesdays. In Dr. Mays' autobiography, *Born to Rebel*, he described Chapel as a "special institution."[99] Reflecting on Mays' influence in Chapel, Dr. Louis Sullivan (class of 1954) stated:

> "(For) virtually all those students during my time, Mays was their role model. He spoke to the students... at Chapel....we looked forward

to his speeches, but beyond his eloquence his words had real substance. He challenged us to be leaders, not to accept the status quo, not to accept desegregation that existed in the South at that time. He inspired us to do the best that we could."[100]

U.S. Congressman from Georgia, Sanford Bishop (class of 1968), was one of many students to receive inspiration and a call to serve from Dr. Mays.

"He planted a seed. He created an atmosphere, which he called in his own words an air of expectancy. In other words when he talked to us in Chapel, he said, 'you're a Morehouse Man, you're not just anybody, you've had this special opportunity to come to Morehouse and be exposed to what we have here on the campus to offer. (As) a Morehouse Man, there is an air of expectancy. You are expected to do well. We expect you to do like those before you, go out and do good in the world, go out and succeed and excel.'"[101]

The Morehouse Man

Benjamin Mays was affectionately called the "Minister of Manhood" by students and alumni, and the ideal student prototype was called the "Morehouse Man." The Morehouse Man was the epitome of excellence in all facets of life, including academics, professional aspirations, family devotion, community service, and leadership. The Morehouse Man was the embodiment of integrity, honesty, respect, resourcefulness, poise, and self-discipline.[102] These were high principles to live up to, and according to Dr. Sullivan, students were transformed by the high expectations and high standards Dr. Mays had of them.

> "What was ingrained in us at that time was high standards...do things well and be sure that you fulfill the expectations that Morehouse has for you. So basically, we had an environment of rigorous scholarship and high expectations that we would go out and change the world. So the competition at Morehouse was who is going to be the best scholar, who is going to show traits of leadership. I think all of that molded us and shaped us, told us to be a leader... that is what was expected."[103]

Commencement and the Graduating Class Challenge

The apex of the academic year was the commencement ceremony. Mays would invite prominent African American leaders such as civil rights icon A. Philip Randolph, U.S. Congressman Adam Clayton Powell, educator Carter G. Woodson, and actor/activist Paul Robeson to speak. These leaders inspired students to follow their examples of service, regardless of where their professional paths would take them after graduation.

Congressman Adam Clayton Powell and Dr. Benjamin E. Mays
in the graduation processional in 1956.
Photo courtesy of the Morehouse College Archives.

During the commencement exercise, Dr. Mays would
issue students a "graduating class challenge" as in the
following excerpt of a speech given in 1958:

> "For good or for ill, from this moment on, you
> will bear the mark, the stamp, the badge of
> Morehouse College. If you attain greatness,
> Morehouse College will attain greatness. If you
> attain mediocrity, Morehouse will be
> mediocre. If you fail in life, and God forbid,

Morehouse College will fail too. Morehouse can be no greater than you, the sum total of the deeds of its alumni.

"Wherever you go, whatever you do, whatever you say, you will carry in your personality, the mark of this college. And never forget that it is expected of Morehouse men that they make their mark in the world—and an honorable mark.

"The eyes of Morehouse College will follow you from now on in. From this moment on you will wear the sign of Morehouse men. Wear it with dignity and pardonable pride."[104]

In another charge to students in 1961, Mays stated:

"May you perform so well that when a man is needed for an important job in your field, your work will be so impressive that the committee of selection will be compelled to examine your credentials. May you forever stand for something noble and high. Let no man dismiss you with a wave of a hand or a shrug of the shoulder. Never forget that you are a Morehouse Man. Good luck and God bless."[105]

Having received their charge from Mays, seniors left their alma mater as Morehouse Men and with a sense of mission and purpose. Mays exhorted alumni to continue the path of excellence and leadership in his "President's Page," a regular feature in *Morehouse Alumnus*, a quarterly magazine published by the college. As Mays said in one issue,

> "We here at Morehouse have but one central aim: to improve the quality and quantity of our work to the end that our graduates will improve the quality of their leadership in their respective communities.

> "...we should strive to produce men superior in poise, social imagination, integrity, resourcefulness, and possessing an all embracing love for all peoples irrespective of race or color"[106]

Nationally Renowned Leaders

(R-L) Georgia State Senators Julian Bond (class of 1971), Horace T. Ward (class of 1949), Leroy Johnson (class of 1949), and an unidentified official. Undated photo courtesy of the Auburn Avenue Research Library of African American Culture & History.

Chapter 3: The Dr. Benjamin E. Mays Era
(1940-1967)

Dr. Mays expected Morehouse students to lead and succeed despite segregation. He urged students to be proud of themselves and stand up for their rights. Mays believed in "...instilling in Morehouse students the idea that despite crippling circumstances the sky was their limit."[107]

The following renowned Morehouse Men are only a few who were inspired by Mays and credit him for their ascension to leadership:

- Dr. Samuel DuBois Cook (class of 1948), the first African American professor at Duke University and the first African American to hold a regular faculty appointment at any predominantly white college or university in the South;
- Lerone Bennett, Jr. (class of 1949), former executive editor of *Ebony* magazine and writer of two historical texts: *Before the Mayflower: A History of Black America, 1619–1962* and *Forced into Glory: Abraham Lincoln's White Dream*;
- Dr. Clinton Warner, Jr. (class of 1949), a civil rights pioneer in Atlanta who initiated a campaign for fair housing and was also a plaintiff in a 1963 lawsuit that desegregated Emory University;
- Donn Clendenon (class of 1956), New York Mets baseball player and 1969 World Series Most Valuable Player (MVP);
- Reginald Eaves (class of 1956), the first African American Commissioner of Public Safety in Atlanta and founding member of the National Organization of Black Law Enforcement Executives (NOBLE);

- Dr. David Satcher (class of 1963), the first African American Surgeon General of the United States;
- Julian Bond (class of 1971), a founding member of the Student Non-Violent Coordinating Committee (SNCC), a former Georgia State Senator, and current Chairman of the Board of the National Association for the Advancement of Colored People (NAACP).

Dr. Benjamin E. Mays' protégé, Atlanta Mayor Maynard H. Jackson (class of 1956) is congratulated by Dr. Hugh M. Gloster. Undated photo from the 1970's Harmon Perry collection, courtesy of the Auburn Avenue Research Library on African American Culture & History.

The Mays Legacy

In 1967, Benjamin Mays retired as president of Morehouse College.

During his 27 years in office, Dr. Mays not only put his indelible stamp on the mission and traditions of Morehouse, he influenced the course of historical events. His

Chapter 3: The Dr. Benjamin E. Mays Era
(1940-1967)

Morehouse Men stared down racism, discrimination, and injustice as government leaders, educators, attorneys, athletes, ministers, and scientists. Three state senators, six state representatives, and presidents at 20 colleges and universities were Morehouse graduates.

Morehouse's endowment was among the highest of all Black colleges under Dr. Mays. Morehouse was one of the few Black colleges selected to establish a Phi Beta Kappa chapter.

As an educator, Dr. Mays taught his students the value of earning advanced degrees. He never accepted the commonly held belief among African Americans of his day that a bachelor's degree was the ultimate goal of higher education. As a result, Morehouse alumni dominated African American enrollment in graduate programs at prestigious colleges and universities.

- During Dr. Mays' presidency, 52 percent of Morehouse seniors attended graduate school:
  - 118 alumni earned Ph.D.'s from Harvard, Yale, Brown, Berkeley, and Ohio State University.
  - One of every eight Morehouse graduates had an academic or professional doctorate (Morehouse Centennial Commencement Program, 1967, p. 2).
  - One of every 18 African Americans nationwide who had earned a Ph.D. was a Morehouse graduate—more than all Black colleges combined.
  - In 1955, 52 of the 737 African Americans enrolled in medical schools were Morehouse alumni.

- Furthermore, by the end of Mays' tenure, the number of Morehouse faculty holding doctorates increased from 3 percent in 1940 to 52 percent in 1967, more than all Black colleges combined.

After his retirement, Dr. Mays remained an active leader, serving in several prominent social and political organizations. He was also in high demand as a speaker and lecturer.

In 1970, Mays was the first African American to be elected as president of the Atlanta Board of Education. He also published two autobiographies in his later years, *Born to Rebel* (1971) and *Lord, the People Have Driven Me On* (1981).

Benjamin Elijah Mays died on March 28, 1984. His funeral was held at the Dr. Martin Luther King, Jr. Chapel on Morehouse's campus to a capacity-filled audience. His remains are buried alongside his wife Sadie on the Morehouse campus, adjacent to Graves Hall. Above his tombstone stands a life-like statue of Dr. Mays; the tombstone, statue, and crypts of Dr. and Mrs. Mays form the Benjamin E. Mays National Memorial. Written on his crypt are the following words, which summarize the essence of his life: "Born to rebel against ignorance, oppression, and social injustice."

Although Dr. Mays did not have any biological children, his exemplary life, persona, and intellect had such an indelible effect on many Morehouse alumni, who proudly and affectionately refer to themselves as "Benny's boys." The Mays legacy is perpetuated by Morehouse College, which has elevated Dr. Benjamin Elijah Mays to the status of an institutional hero. He is memorialized through frequent references of his quotes, life-like pictures that are strategically placed throughout campus, and the naming of a residence hall.

Chapter 3: The Dr. Benjamin E. Mays Era
(1940-1967)

The influence of Mays, however, goes beyond Morehouse College. His name is synonymous with academic excellence, and many schools, scholarship funds, and academies across the United States bear his name.

President Mays' farewell address at the 1967 Morehouse College Commencement marked the ceremonial end of his Morehouse presidency. The following excerpt memorializes his belief in the mission of Morehouse in his own words:

> "Now my dear Seniors, let me say to you what I said to the graduating class of 1964. Will you please rise?

> The curtain has fallen forever on the activities of your years at Morehouse. What you have done, poorly or well, can never be erased. What you should have done and neglected to do cannot now be done. Not even an omnipotent God can blot the deeds of history. It has been beautifully said:

> 'The Moving Finger writes: and having writ, Moves on; nor all your piety nor Wit Shall lure it back to cancel half a line, Nor all your Tears wash out a word of it.'

> Since the events of history are irrevocable, I can only advise you to utilize the past, whatever it is, to good advantage and to look to the future with courage and confidence.

Wherever I may be 25 years from today…you will make my spirit glad if you are known in life by the quality of your work and the integrity of your character, rather than by the quantity of your possessions.

If you do the ordinary work of the world, do it with distinction and make no apology for it, for all work is honorable, if it is beneficial to mankind.

My dear young friends, I do not know what happiness is and I do not think it is important that you be happy. But it is important that you find your work and do it as if you were sent into the world at this precise moment in history to do your job. If happiness can be achieved, it will be found in a job well done and in giving and not receiving."[108]

Chapter 4: Dr. Martin Luther King, Jr.

"At some point in your life we expect you to be Dr. Martin Luther King, not just a great minister, not just a great preacher, but someone who is changing, who leaves a foot print. I can't think of any other environment, for my generation, where the focus would be on telling black men—you can be that powerful, world changing."[109]

Dr. Michael Lomax (class of 1968)
President/CEO, United Negro College Fund

The Fulfillment of the Messianic Hope

The concept of "messianic hope" is deeply embedded in the Judeo-Christian heritage of African Americans. They have believed that God would send them someone who would deliver them from the oppression and suffering of slavery and beyond. This deliverer would bring freedom from their oppressors through revolutionary means.

An educational institution with deep roots in the Black Baptist tradition, Morehouse College too has espoused this liberation theology. Inherent in its mission is the belief that alumni will become leaders and help deliver those who are oppressed. For many, Dr. Martin Luther King, Jr., a champion of civil and human rights and arguably one of the most influential people of the 20th century, was a fulfillment of this messianic hope.

Morehouse College played an indisputable yet underappreciated role in King's development as a leader who would one day galvanize the civil rights movement and inspire human rights activists around the world. This chapter is devoted to Dr. Martin Luther King, Jr. because of his social and political activism, his heroic accomplishments, and his eventual martyrdom, all of which grew out of the legacy of leadership that has become the hallmark of the Morehouse College mission.

On February 18, 1946, Dr. Benjamin Mays made the following prophetic statement on a live radio address on WGST radio in Atlanta:

> "If we should lift out of Atlanta, the contribution that Morehouse Men are making in the fields of religion, medicine, education, business, journalism, social work, race relations and good citizenship, Atlanta would be much poorer. What is true of Atlanta would be true of the major cities of the South and in many small towns and rural areas...and in many sections in the East and West.
>
> But we are not complacent. We are disturbed about man and about the state of the world. Morehouse's greatest contribution to Atlanta, to the South, and to the nation is yet to be made. It will not be the purpose of the college to produce mere scholars or men technically trained...Morehouse dedicates itself in the years to come to the development of spiritual skills: skills in the art of living together in harmony and good will—black men, white men, red men, yellow men, brown men...."[110]

The Morehouse Years

Among the many students greatly influenced by Dr. Benjamin Mays was Martin Luther King, Jr., for as a Morehouse student and throughout his adult years, King would embrace Mays' prophetic message of racial harmony for the betterment of humanity.

King's selection of Morehouse as his college of choice was no accident. In the 1940's, Morehouse College was considered to be the best college for African American males, and King's family ties to the college were strong. His grandfather, Rev. Adam Daniel (A.D.) Williams (class of 1898), his father, Rev. Martin L. King, Sr. (class of 1930), and his younger brother, A.D. Williams King (class of 1960), were all graduates of Morehouse. Meanwhile, his mother, Alberta Williams King, attended Spelman Seminary (high school). His older sister, Christine, graduated from Spelman College the same day in 1948 as King, Jr. graduated from Morehouse.

Fulfilling his destiny to become a third generation Morehouse Man, King, Jr. enrolled on September 20, 1944 without fanfare in the early admission program at the age of 15. According to Dr. Mays, "He was just one freshman among many others."[111] However, during King's four year matriculation at Morehouse, a series of factors undeniably influenced his development as a leader.

Like his fellow classmates, King experienced the academic rigors of Morehouse, but he was an average student. He graduated with a 2.48 grade point average and a Bachelor's in sociology on June 8, 1948. King later expounded on the academic challenges he encountered at Morehouse in one of his speeches:

"When I was in college, I had to take a course that was required called statistics. And statistics can be very complicated and I had a fellow classmate who could just work that stuff out. He could do his homework in about an hour. We would often go to the lab...and he would just work it out in about an hour, and it was over for him. And I was trying to do what he was doing (by) trying to do mine in an hour. And the more I tried to do it in an hour, the more I was flunking out in the course."[112]

Although King, Jr. lived at home during his entire college career, he described his college days as "very exciting ones"[113] and spent sufficient time on campus to develop strong friendships with his peers, participate in the joint social activities of Morehouse College and Spelman College, and establish a close relationship with Morehouse faculty and staff. Describing the academic and social climate at Morehouse, King stated,

"There was a free atmosphere at Morehouse, and it was there I had my first frank discussion on race. The professors were not caught up in the clutches of state funds and could teach what they wanted with academic freedom. They encouraged us in a positive quest for a solution to racial ills. I realized that nobody there was afraid. Important people came in to discuss the race problem rationally with us."[114]

Among the many people encountered by King, he was greatly influenced by Dr. Mays, referring to him as his "intellectual father" and "spiritual mentor." King was inspired by his talks in Chapel, and he would often follow Mays to his office afterwards to discuss the topics that were presented.[115]

King also had a good relationship with his religion professor, Dr. George Kelsey (class of 1934), who taught in the Religion and Philosophy Department. In 1956, King disclosed that both Mays and Kelsey inspired him to enter the ministry, stating "I could see in their lives the ideal of what I wanted a minister to be."[116] Kelsey's emphasis on the Christian gospel as the basis for social reform appealed to King and helped bridge the gap between religion and secular ideas. After taking Kelsey's course, King reflected that "behind the legends and myths of the Book were many profound truths which one could not escape."[117]

While King did not demonstrate academic proficiency during his time at Morehouse, he was very active in extracurricular activities, which honed his extraordinary leadership abilities. King served as president of the sociology club and was a member of the debate team, student council, Glee Club, and minister's union. Judge Horace T. Ward described King as a "big man on campus" who emerged as a leader among the "Atlanta group" of students.[118] King was well liked by his classmates and was affectionately referred to as "M.L." or "tweed," a nickname dating back to his junior high days that recalled his snappy attire and tweed jackets. King joined the Morehouse chapter of the NAACP and played on the Morehouse intramural basketball team (the "City Slickers") and the Butler Street YMCA basketball team. King participated in the annual John L. Webb oratorical competition, winning second prize in 1946 and 1948, demonstrating early on his strong oratorical ability.

Like his peers, King was exposed to a plethora of ideas presented by the parade of speakers at daily Chapel. Leroy Johnson (class of 1949) believes that King embraced the same "call to service" that other students accepted as they became keenly aware of social and political issues of the day.[119]

King's school activities propelled him towards the ministry and the struggle for civil rights, as evident in his writings during his Morehouse years. The summer before his junior year, King wrote the editor of the *Atlanta Constitution* newspaper on August 6, 1946 to respond to a series of racially motivated murders in Georgia. In the letter, King summarized the goals of African American citizens:

> "We want and are entitled to the basic rights and opportunities of American citizens: The right to earn a living at work for which we are fitted by training and ability; equal opportunities in education, health, recreation, and similar public services; the right to vote; equality before the law; some of the same courtesy and good manners that we ourselves bring to all human relations."[120]

During his junior year, King wrote an article for the *Maroon Tiger*, the school newspaper, entitled, "The Purpose of Education." In this article, King warned his Morehouse peers about misconceptions regarding the purpose of education and asserted what he believed was the true function of education:

"It seems to me that education has a two-fold
function to perform in the life of man and in
society: the one is utility and the other is
culture. Education must enable a man to
become more efficient, to achieve with
increasing facility the legitimate goals of his
life. Education must also train one for quick,
resolute and effective thinking. To think
incisively and to think for ones self is very
difficult."[121]

These commentaries reflected King's growing awareness of
social issues, the depth of his intellectual curiosity, and his
commitment to fighting racial injustice.

The summer prior to King's senior year was pivotal
in his journey to the ministry. His sister, Christine, reflected,
"…at first, he thought about being a doctor, then he became
serious about the ministry, started reading the Bible, and
avoided going to parties…"[122] Childhood friend and Spelman
student June Dobbs Butts attended a class with King. She
observed that "He shared very visionary and prophetic ideas
and went through a metamorphosis."[123]

King's involvement with the Intercollegiate Council
of Atlanta, an interracial student group that met monthly to
discuss various social issues, also strengthened his resolve.
Working together with white students helped him overcome
his own "anti-white feelings." King recalled,

"I had been ready to resent the whole white
race, but as I got to see more of white people,
my resentment was softened, and a spirit of

cooperation took its place. I was at the point where I was deeply interested in political matters and social ills. I could envision myself playing a part in breaking down the legal barriers to Negro rights."[124]

In the fall of his senior year, King, Jr. told his father that he had decided to enter the ministry. King, Jr. preached his trial sermon at Ebenezer Baptist Church, was ordained on February 25, 1948, and became an associate pastor. King, Sr. was the pastor of Ebenezer, the historic church on Auburn Avenue and where grandfather King also had served as pastor.

Prior to his graduation from Morehouse in 1948, King, like many of his classmates, considered graduate study. He applied to Crozer Theological Seminary of Chester, Pennsylvania. His mentor, Dr. Kelsey, wrote the following recommendation to Crozer officials:

"The academic rigor of Martin Luther King, Jr. is short of what can be called good but I recommend you give his application serious consideration. King is one of those boys who came to realize the value of scholarship late in his college career. His ability exceeds his record at Morehouse, and I believe his present attitude will lift his achievement to the level of his ability. He presently is being quite serious about the ministry as a calling rather than a profession. His record of citizenship at Morehouse is good."[125]

Martin L. King, Jr. graduation photo with the class of 1948.
Photo courtesy of the Morehouse College Archives

The Graduate School Years

Crozer accepted King in 1948, and as Dr. Kelsey predicted, his Morehouse experience had prepared him to meet the challenge of graduate studies. As one of only six African Americans among a study body of 100, King was competing for the first time with whites.[126] Yet, he rose to the occasion and was so respected by his classmates and faculty that in 1951, that he was elected student body president, which, according to Crozer Seminary Dean Charles E. Bratten was a "position of great responsibility."[127] Bratten wrote in a letter to Dr. Benjamin E. Mays the following progress report of Martin King's academic work and leadership at Crozer:

King is one of the most outstanding students from my point of view. Academically he is doing superior work. He is held universally in high regard by faculty, staff, and students, and is undoubtedly one of the best men in our entire student body. He reflects fine preparation, an excellent mind, and a thorough grasp of material."[128]

While at Crozer, King attended a lecture by Howard University president, Morehouse alumnus, and former protégé of Dr. John Hope, Dr. Mordecai W. Johnson at the Fellowship House in Philadelphia. King listened to a message on Gandhi "so profound and electrifying" that he was compelled to buy "a half-dozen books."[129] King was mesmerized by Gandhi's ideology and began reading profusely about his life and philosophy.

King rose to the top of his class and in 1951, was named valedictorian. He earned a Bachelor of Divinity Degree and won both the Peral Plafkner Award for scholarship and the Lewis Crozer Fellowship for further graduate study.

King went on to pursue a Ph.D. in Systematic Theology at Boston University. While completing his studies in 1953, he developed a close relationship with another fellow Morehouse alumnus and John Hope protégé, Dr. Howard Thurman, the recently appointed Dean of Marsh Chapel and Professor of Spiritual Disciplines and Resources at Boston University. In later years, Thurman would become one of King's confidants. Thurman's 1949 book, *Jesus and the Disinherited,* interprets Jesus' teachings through the experience of the oppressed, and it proposed a nonviolent response to oppression. King relied on the book for strength and guidance during the Montgomery boycott.

Chapter 4: Dr. Martin Luther King Jr.

The Civil Rights Movement

Throughout his graduate school years, King maintained a close relationship with Dr. Benjamin Mays. After completing his studies at Boston University, Mays offered King a teaching position at Morehouse. King chose instead to become pastor of the Dexter Avenue Baptist Church in Montgomery, Alabama. There, in 1955, he made his first mark on the modern civil rights movement by mobilizing the Black community in a 382-day boycott of the city's bus lines. Dr. Mays, along with King's many family, friends, and associates, supported him during those challenging times.[130]

After the success of the historic boycott, King became a national hero and a civil rights figure of growing importance. In 1957, King laid the groundwork for the organization now known as the Southern Christian Leadership Conference (SCLC). He was elected its first president, and he soon began helping other communities organize their own protests against racial discrimination.

In recognition of his leadership in the boycott, Morehouse College became the first college or university in America to bestow an honorary doctorate on Dr. King (June 1957). Dr. Mays, filled with fatherly pride, said it "gave him great joy to confer the degree" upon his protégé."[131]

In 1960, King returned to Atlanta to serve as co-pastor of Ebenezer Baptist Church with his father. In 1963, he was a major organizer of the historic March on Washington, where he delivered his famous "I Have a Dream" speech. That same year, *Time* magazine named him "Person of the Year," and in 1964, he was awarded the Nobel Peace Prize. Morehouse College again gave tribute, and for many years, King's medal was housed in the faculty lounge of Samuel Howard Archer Hall.

71

Continuing Ties with Morehouse College

King frequently returned to Morehouse, where he made an unforgettable impression on students. In 1965, King was elected to serve as a Morehouse College trustee. He hosted town hall meetings on campus and joined Morehouse students in sit-in demonstrations at segregated department stores in downtown Atlanta. Remarking on King's influence on Morehouse students during this period, Congressman Sanford Bishop said,

> "My freshman year Dr. Martin Luther King received the Nobel Prize, and I got to meet him. Dr. Mays conferred an honorary degree on him at convocation. I was exposed to this great historic figure and from that point I began to follow him and almost to become a disciple. For the next 3½ years he was like an idol...."[132]

Dr. Benjamin E. Mays followed by Dr. Martin Luther King, Jr. in the Morehouse Commencement processional (1965). Photo courtesy of the Morehouse College Archives.

The Martyrdom of King

Mays and King had formed a pact that whoever died first, the other would give his eulogy. Tragically, King was assassinated on April 4, 1968, in Memphis, Tennessee. His death caused a wave of violence in major cities across the country, including Atlanta.

On April 9, 1968, Dr. King's private funeral was held at Ebenezer Baptist Church. Afterwards, King's mahogany coffin, placed on a rickety farm wagon pulled by two mules, journeyed to Morehouse College for the public outdoor funeral, where Dr. Mays delivered an electrifying eulogy from the steps of Harkness Hall, the administration building Morehouse shared with Atlanta University. Dr. Benjamin Mays, president emeritus and mentor of King, spoke before a crowd of approximately 150,000 mourners. He said, "Martin Luther King, Jr. believed in a united America. He believed that the walls of separation brought on by legal and de facto segregation, and discrimination based on race could be eradicated."[133] Dr. Mays declared what everyone in attendance knew to be true: "Surely this man was called of God to do this work. Martin Luther King, Jr. was a prophet in the twentieth century. Martin Luther King was called of God to prophesy in his time."[134]

President Emeritus Dr. Benjamin E. Mays delivers King's eulogy.

Many Morehouse students and alumni were present at King's funeral. Congressman Sanford Bishop, president of the Student Government Association at the time, vividly recalled that fateful day:

> "I walked with the mule train that pulled his body through the campus, I sang in the funeral, in the Glee Club, that was heavy; an awesome experience. And to have all the national and international dignitaries come to the campus and walk over there. ...-- It was unbelievable."[135]

Another Morehouse student who was greatly influenced by King's death and funeral was Dr. Roderic Pettigrew (class of 1972), the current First Director, National Institute of Biomedical Imaging and Bioengineering.

"During... my freshman year, campus life changed for all of us when Morehouse alumnus, Dr. Martin Luther King, Jr. was assassinated. I was grief stricken by the news of his death, fearful of potential broader similar acts of violent hatred, and became particularly concerned for the well being of my closest friend at Spelman College to the point of seeking her out to provide safe haven.

A few days later, we attended Dr. King's funeral on the Morehouse campus and heard an inspiring eulogy given by Morehouse president emeritus, Dr. Benjamin Mays. He shared how Dr. King and he had made a pact that whoever died first would be eulogized by the survivor of the two.

As we left the funeral and joined the solemn procession from the Morehouse campus to the grave site, I reflected on this powerful display of friendship and mutual respect that these two great Black men had for one another. Dr Mays then, as he did on many occasions, spoke of the Morehouse tradition and expectation that its graduates go into the world and distinguish

75

themselves through contributions that change the world for the better. Several of us (including my classmate and compatriot Calvin Butts III), resolved and would often restate our desire to make an impact in society like them; each of us in his own special way."[136]

Fellow alumnus, Maynard Jackson (class of 1956), saw King's death as a "summons for action."[137] Jackson was so moved by the assassination that he quit his law practice and decided to challenge the incumbent United States Senator Herman Talmadge from Georgia. Although Jackson lost that race, his showing was impressive. He proved to himself and others that Georgia was ready for an African American political leader. In 1969, Jackson was elected Atlanta's first Vice Mayor; in 1973, he was elected the city's first African American mayor.

Another person affected by King's assassination was current Morehouse College president Dr. Robert Michael Franklin (class of 1975). Franklin stated, "(My dad) told me to sit and watch the funeral ceremony of Dr. King (on television). After watching the ceremony together, my dad looked at me and said: 'That's where I'd like you to go to college'"[138]

The King Legacy

Dr. Martin Luther King, Jr. was arguably one of the most influential leaders of the 20th century. His life and works have had an immeasurable impact on many aspects of American life.

Chapter 4: Dr. Martin Luther King Jr.

King was a friend and role model for Morehouse students. He left an indelible mark on students, inspiring them to serve as change agents in their communities. Following the death of Dr. King, Jr., the King family and Morehouse College grew closer. Martin Luther King, III (class of 1979) and Dexter Scott King (1979–1984) both attended Morehouse. His daughter, Bernice Albertine King, is a graduate of Spelman, and his wife, Coretta, served as a Morehouse trustee and was a frequent convocation speaker as early as Commencement 1970.

To honor Dr. King's memory, Morehouse erected the Martin Luther King, Jr. International Chapel in 1978, which adjoins the Gloster Hall administration building. The Chapel is the largest religious monument to King found anywhere in the world. The King Chapel has a large, imposing statue of Dr. King on the grounds near the front entrance. The monument inscription reads:

"From Morehouse College he launched his humanitarian pilgrimage to create the beloved community, and for that purpose he moved out from the classroom and his pulpit to march his way into immortality."

While King died prematurely at the age of 39, his impact on Morehouse is timeless. He bore the endearing qualities of the quintessential Morehouse Man: intelligence, compassion, integrity, courage, and a commitment to the underserved.

Under the influence of the Morehouse Mystique, King thrived and matured. His awareness of societal ills was enhanced by daily Chapel and the rigors of the classroom;

and he was the beneficiary of close mentoring relationships with Mays, Kelsey, Johnson, and Thurman. His leadership qualities were nurtured through his involvement in campus activities that were available to all students.

Conversely, Morehouse College has used the life of Dr. Martin Luther King, Jr. to strengthen and substantiate its mission as a developer of leaders. King is hailed in the Morehouse community as a role model and hero.

PART 2

The Transformational Experience

Photo courtesy of Morehouse College, Office of Communications

Chapter 5: The State of
African American Males in Education

Unidentified Morehouse student.
Undated photo courtesy of Morehouse College

As a predominantly Black, private, liberal arts college for men, Morehouse College is the only institution of its kind in the United States. Its exclusive status and remarkable track record of producing prominent alumni make Morehouse College a repository of proven successful strategies for developing African American males into responsible, creative, and productive men.

For the past 30 years, many studies have been devoted to measuring the impact of the college environment on student learning and cognitive development.[139] A central question posed in many of these studies has been: "What evidence do we have that different colleges and universities have a differential influence on learning and cognitive development?"[2] According to some, most of the outcome achievement differences among students are attributable to pre-college characteristics. For example, educational researcher Alexander Astin asserted that "The quality of the student's academic preparation at the time of entry proved to have more frequent and stronger relationships to most outcome measures than any other single category of freshman or environmental variable."[141]

Other studies show that at historically Black colleges and universities, outcome achievement differences are attributable to environmental factors. Black post-secondary schools are perceived and characterized by African American students as friendly, socially accommodating, and hospitable, which positively affect students' academic performance. Research performed by Patricia Gurin and Edgar Epps found that African American students who attend Black schools possess positive self-images, strong racial pride, and high aspirations.[142]

Environmental differences also account for outcome achievement differences at single-sex institutions. Several studies found that students who attend single-sex institutions experience greater gains than those who attend coed colleges.[143]

Morehouse College possesses many of the environmental factors found in Black colleges as well as single-sex colleges that positively impact students' academic achievement and aspirations for professional success. The present study's qualitative and quantitative research affirms that Morehouse students are career-minded, self-confident, and leadership-oriented. They possess a missionary zeal, have racial pride, value academic excellence, and embrace brotherhood.

Chapter 5: The State of African American Males in Education

The manner in which Morehouse students benefit from their collegiate experience is akin to the manner in which African American male primary and secondary students benefit from a homogeneous classroom environment.[144] Early studies found that African American males in single-sex schools benefit greatly from this type of environment because of the focus on Afrocentrism, the high level of teacher expectations, and the enforcement of discipline.[145] Reinforced by the growing research evidence in support of the merits of an African American single-sex education, the Morehouse administration and its alumni base have resisted the suggestion that Morehouse College become co-educational.

Compared to the universe of primary, secondary, and post-secondary schools in America, Morehouse College, however, has "something more" as Addie Butler wrote in her book, *The Distinctive Black College: Talladega, Tuskegee, and Morehouse* [146] as well as "an intangible something" as Mays described in his autobiography, *Born to Rebel*.[147] This something more is a combination of interrelated and connected components within the distinctive Morehouse Mystique that provides a centering orientation of development for students. These components are the rich leadership legacy, the air of expectancy, the self-esteem building through messaging, the mentoring by faculty and staff, the bond of brotherhood, the modeling of the Morehouse Man, and the climate of celebration. These components, which are so intricately embedded into the fiber of the college, can and must be applied to primary, secondary, and post-secondary schools across America to counteract the crisis of African American males in education.

A Call to Action

David Hefner wrote in his article, "Where the boys aren't" that: "The decline of Black males in colleges and universities has sociologists and educators concerned about the future of the African American community."[148] As evident from the following statistics, Hefner's concern has merit. From 1980 to 2000, African American enrollment growth in higher education has been "extraordinarily slow" when compared to other groups by race, ethnicity, and gender. For example, African American male enrollment in colleges and universities grew from 464,000 in 1980 to 635,000 by the beginning of the 2000 fall semester. This 37 percent increase, however, pales in comparison to African American females whose enrollment was 643,000 in 1980 yet nearly doubled 20 years later to 1.1 million. This translates to approximately 450,000 fewer African American males enrolled in college than African American females in 2000.[149]

The disparity, however, is not limited to college enrollment, but it is particularly acute between African American males' and females' college completion rates. For example, in 1980, 24,511 African American men earned bachelor's degrees, compared to 36,162 African American women, a disparity of 11,651. Twenty years later, the disparity more than tripled when 38,103 African American men earned bachelor's degrees nationwide compared to 73,204 African American women. By 2000, there was a disconcerting disparity of African American graduates: 70 percent of African American college graduates were women, while only 30 percent were men.

Chapter 5: The State of
African American Males in Education

African American Males: Endangered or Ignored?

The growing educational disparity among African Americans is the result of the steady achievement gains of females against the backdrop of dismal educational gains for males since 1980. Compared to their female counterparts, African American males lag behind throughout the entire educational pipeline from elementary, to secondary, and to post-secondary levels. More than any group by race, ethnicity, and gender, African American males are most likely to be suspended or expelled from school; and with the exception of Latino males, they are most likely to be high school dropouts. They also are underrepresented in gifted education programs and advanced placement courses. They are most likely to be academic underachievers in terms of grade performance, a problem that becomes most acute by the fourth grade. Additionally, they experience many challenges and hurdles in higher education, resulting in higher attrition rates.[150]

Given the growing disparity of college access, academic achievement, and degree attainment, African American males are characterized today by such disparaging terms as endangered, dysfunctional, dangerous, and uneducable. The disparity in educational attainment and achievement among African American males, compared to females and students from other ethnic groups, is attributable to a multitude of reasons, including the following:

Prison Incarceration. At the beginning of 2008, the United States had the highest incarceration rates by both raw numbers (2.3 million) and percentage of the general population (750 per 100,000) than any other country in the entire world.[151] The American criminal justice system adversely affects college access, for there are more African American males in the U.S.

85

prison population than there are enrolled in American colleges and universities.

While African American juveniles make up 15 percent of the general population of adolescents, they make up 43 percent of the juvenile population in public facilities and 34 percent in private custody facilities.[152] One out of every 21 African Americans aged 18 and over is imprisoned, and for African American males aged 20 to 34, the ratio of free African Americans to those imprisoned is startling: one in nine is in jail or prison.[153] As a result, African American men in their early 30s are nearly two times more likely to have been incarcerated than to have earned a bachelor's degree.[154]

From these imposing statistics we see that a disproportionate number of African American male adolescents are represented in the criminal justice system, which decreases their chances of going to college and makes them less likely to be fully active and productive citizens.

Mortality Rates. Turn on any television news program and during the first 15 minutes, the reports will focus on African American males as victims and perpetrators of crime. This is both a problem of perception and reality for African American males. The overrepresentation of African American males in criminal activity, amplified by the portrayal in the media, leads to the stereotype that *all* African American males are lawless and susceptible to criminal activity. While most African Americans do not resort to crime, the fact remains that far too many are involved in criminal activity, which leads to incarceration and premature deaths.

According to the U.S. Department of Justice, homicide is the leading cause of death among young African American males. African American males 18 to 24 years of age had the highest homicide offending rate among all races and ethnicities in 2005—more than three times the rate of African American males ages 14 to 17 years and almost five times the rate of African American males ages 25 and older. African American males ages 18 to 24 years also had the highest homicide victimization rate in 2005—more than double the rate for African American males ages 25 and older and almost four times the rate for African American males ages 14 to 17 years old.[155]

Inadequate Education. African American males have excessive rates of suspension in elementary and secondary school compared to females and males from other ethnic groups.[156] While African Americans make up 17 percent of the total school population, they account for 32 percent of the suspensions and 30 percent of all expulsions—most of these disciplinary cases involved African American males.[157]

Furthermore, African American male teens are placed in remedial or special education classes at triple the rate of their white counterparts,[158] and they are underrepresented in gifted and honors classes. African American males experience lower high school graduation rates than African American females and males from other ethnic groups; and they attain low overall mean achievement scores for standardized tests, compared to females and males from other ethnic groups.[159] Nationally, African American males have a 42 percent chance of dropping out of high school,[160] and 52 percent of African American men born between 1965 and 1969 who were high school dropouts as teens went to prison by their 30s (ages 30–34).[161]

African American males face other unique challenges that may compromise their success in school. They are susceptible to negative imagery and stereotyping. Negative stereotyping, perpetuated by the media, can shape the perceptions and expectations of principals and teachers. Teachers' low expectations often lead to student disengagement which, in turn, lowers the teachers' expectations, further exacerbating a vicious cycle downward. African American males who internalize such negative beliefs about themselves become self-destructive and compromise their educational success.

The Glamour of Athletics. On any given day in America—during school hours, after-school, on holidays, and summer vacations—one can hear and see young African American males bouncing basketballs, ready to play, and ready to challenge each other for the title of "the greatest." This is true of athletics in general, though primarily basketball, football, and occasionally baseball. The glamour of basketball, football and to a lesser degree baseball has led many African American males to disdain education as "white" and "anti-Black." This makes it terribly difficult for school officials and community leaders to direct their energies toward the nobler pursuits of education. Few African American males will achieve stardom as professional athletes; and most who achieve it will retire from the playing field—worn, old, and broken—without real and lasting skills to support themselves or their families.

Shamefully, too often the only role models visible to African American males are athletes who are glorified in the mainstream media. Many young African Americans males believe that their only path to success is through athletics. Lindsey Luebchow wrote in his article, "Minority Recruitment: Athletics Success, Admissions Failure," that "If colleges don't actively recruit (African Americans) for academic achievement and potential, that perception becomes a reality in many high schools throughout the country."[162] Unfortunately, a disproportionately high number of African Americans enroll in colleges and universities as athletes. This is our loss as a society. The souls and minds of African American males are precious, not disposable, and every effort should be made to challenge the various social stereotypes and push African American males towards academic excellence.

Implications for Parents, Educators, and Policy Makers

Education is considered by many to be the great equalizer within American society. The thinking goes that despite one's economic status in life, education can theoretically allow one to climb the social and economic ladder to success. The reality, however, is that the lower one is on the social and economic ladder, the harder it is to climb.

Historically, middle-class and some working class fathers within African American communities have been the principal breadwinners of families. In contemporary times, fathers, coupled with stronger and more independent mothers, make optimal efforts to sustain families. Single-parent, female-headed households among African Americans have grown tremendously since 1965. There is a strong correlation between economic standing and educational attainment, so it behooves African American parents to embrace and place a high premium on the education of their children.

African Americans, however, must be cognizant of the negative forces, both real and imaged within American society, that inhibit African American males in their pursuit of education. The statistical evidence is undeniable. Noted educator, Jawanza Kunjufu demonstrated how African American boys and girls enter the first grade of elementary school with enthusiasm and a love of learning; however, by the fourth grade, there is a noticeable slowdown in enthusiasm and interest in school by African American boys, compared to African American girls.[163] As African American boys progress along the educational pipeline from elementary school to high school, their attrition rates are higher than African American girls. African American boys are more likely to display problem behaviors and suffer suspensions or expulsions. They also are more likely to be tracked in low academically performing classes than African American girls, and they are more likely to drop out of school.

African American parents must play a hands-on approach to instilling the importance of education in the hearts and minds of their sons. School psychologist and author James Comer emphasized the importance of parental involvement in children's education at home and school to ensure academic success. He wrote,

"Children who grow up in stimulating, emotionally supportive, highly verbal, and protective environments where the caretaker teaches and models skill development are usually ready for school. When the child is able to meet expectations, he or she receives praise or a positive feedback in school. This also compliments the caretaker—a child-rearing job well done. The caretaker or parent and school people feel good about each other. The child receives a message from parents that the school program is good. The positive emotional bond between parents and child is extended to the school. The school staff can then serve as parent surrogates. This facilitates learning."[164]

Additionally, parents must help their sons develop a more realistic perspective about sports. While sports are excellent at instilling teamwork, personal responsibility, a strong work ethic, discipline, and self-initiative, sports should never supplant education as the goal of life. Sadly, some African American parents have discouraged education as an "uppity" experience and are more inclined to attend a school's athletic event than a Parent Teacher Association (PTA) meeting or a scheduled teacher-parent conference—and their sons take note. African American boys cannot live on athletics alone. They need a solid foundation based on education and skills development.

The continued disparities of academic performance and achievement among African American males in relation to African American females will have dire consequences in the future for families and the Black community. As stated earlier, African American males are outdistanced and outperformed by African American females at every stage of the educational pipeline from elementary school to college. The traditional dual parent family structure of a man and woman will continue to erode as African American females encounter a shrinking pool of available African American males as potential marriage partners. This will be especially the case for African American women on the higher end of the educational spectrum.

The shrinking flow of African American males along the educational pipeline is most acutely observed on the college level. African American males constitute approximately 36.4 percent of all African Americans enrolled in American colleges compared to African American females. Due to greater attrition among African American males, their graduation rate is only 30 percent of the total of African Americans who graduate with a bachelor's degree.

This disparity is most pronounced on Black college campuses. Howard University, one of the premier schools in the country that receives thousands of applications from eager students each year, is experiencing a problem that many other colleges are experiencing—the low enrollment of African American males. In 2007, Howard University President H. Patrick Swygert stated: "Of the 10,500 students enrolled in the university, 65% of our university students are women, so it's more than a two to one [female to male] ratio again."[165] Howard University is not alone. Listed below is the enrollment breakdown by gender among a representative sample of Black colleges:

School	Female	Male
Fisk University	72%	28%
Tuskegee University	60%	40%
Clark Atlanta University	72%	26%
Hampton University	60%	40%
Florida A&M University	56%	44%
St. Paul's College	63%	37%
Virginia State University	58%	42%
St. Augustine's College	58%	42%
Lincoln University	57%	43%
Dillard University	78%	28%

(Source: *College: Where Are The Black Males?*)

This male-to-female disparity has social and academic ramifications. The small pool of African American males puts undue social pressure on African American females in terms of enjoying such social opportunities as dating and learning to manage relationships with their male counterparts. On the other hand, African American males, due to their low numbers, can experience social and academic isolation, particularly on predominantly white campuses. Diversity that is so warmly embraced within the college community lacks richness because of the low presence of African American males. African American males are also less likely to participate in leadership roles outside of athletics and less socially engaged in campus activities on Black and white college campuses.

African American male students who drop out of schools or underachieve are a tragedy and a burden on society. The ability to earn income impacts the economic and social structures of families and local communities. African American male dropouts are more likely to resort to criminal activities, less likely to have permanent or high paying jobs, less likely to be married, and more likely to be absentee fathers. Consequently, mothers too frequently must bear the load of caring and providing for their children alone.

Each of these problems creates a multiplier effect in communities across the country and strains health and human services programs, which are taxed to their limits. The criminal justice system, another benefactor of tax dollars from county and municipal governments, is also overloaded.

Meanwhile, boards of education at the municipal, county, and state levels are under heightening pressure from tax payers, parents, and proponents of pubic education to show better test results and increase graduation rates.

The Morehouse Mystique

Within this overwhelmingly gloomy picture, however, there is an oasis of hope. There is one post-secondary institution in America that is head and shoulders above the rest in terms of consistently engaging, educating, and empowering African American males. Morehouse students today are cultivated in the Morehouse Mystique. They are encouraged to embrace brotherhood among fellow students and alumni. They are also challenged to minister to the less fortunate. Morehouse students are urged to reach their academic potential, attain a terminal degree, assume leadership roles after graduation, and excel in their respective professional fields. In the spirit of Dr. Mays, Morehouse Men are challenged to leave the world better off than when they found it.

Chapter 6: From Boys to Men – The Morehouse Mystique

"It will not be sufficient for Morehouse College
to produce clever graduates,
men fluent in speech; but rather honest men, men who can
be trusted both in public and private life—men who are
sensitive to the wrongs, the sufferings,
and the injustices of society, and who are willing to accept
responsibility for correcting ills."[166]

Dr. Benjamin E. Mays
Morehouse College President

Deal and Peterson in their book, *Shaping School Culture,* define school culture as a "powerful web of rituals and traditions, norms, and values that affects every corner of school life."[167] While every school has its own special culture, Morehouse College has a distinctive institutional culture, frequently referred to as the Morehouse Mystique. This mystique, which empowers and inspires students to aspire towards greatness, contains the following seven interrelated components:

1. A rich legacy of leadership
2. An air of expectancy
3. Self-esteem building through messaging
4. Mentoring by faculty and staff
5. A bond of brotherhood
6. Modeling of the Morehouse Man
7. A climate of celebration

The Morehouse Mystique

Thus far, we have discussed leadership—leadership development in students and the modeling of leadership by faculty, administration, and alumni—and the high expectations of students. In chapter 8 (Perspectives of Presidents, Faculty, and Staff), we will look at how faculty and staff are charged with the mandate to mentor and motivate students. Just as students are expected to do great things, their instructors and the administration are expected to go the extra mile for students. From the president to the students, the entire Morehouse family is held to the highest of standards.

In this chapter we will further deconstruct the Morehouse Mystique by examining Self-Esteem Building Through Messaging, A Bond of Brotherhood, Modeling of the Morehouse Man, and A Climate of Celebration.

Self-Esteem Building Through Messaging

There is power in positive reinforcement, which can impact a student's confidence and satisfaction—in other words, a student's self-esteem. Morehouse masterfully builds the self-esteem and identity of students through a consistent flow of positive messages and affirmations. As noted by Morehouse College professor and historian Edward A. Jones (class of 1926),

> "...since its...beginnings (Morehouse) ...has been dedicated to the task of building men: first by enlightening their minds then by freeing them from the shackles of a psychological conditioning brought about by nearly two hundred years of slavery."[168]

Chapter 6: From Boys to Men – The Morehouse
Mystique

Similarly, Dr. Mays noted that after 1920, Morehouse helped students realize they "could do big and worthwhile things."[169] In his farewell address in 1967, Dr. Mays said,

> "If Morehouse graduates...have done better than the graduates of most predominantly Negro colleges, it is due in part to the philosophy drilled into them that the Morehouse Man can succeed in the world despite crippling circumstances under which he had to live."[170]

Students receive this systematic barrage of positive messages from freshman year through graduation.

In her cross-comparative research of American colleges and universities, Jacqueline Fleming found that "Morehouse seems to have an impact on its students that is positive and well-rounded."[171] Additionally, Betty Burney of Jacksonville, Florida, who currently has a son at the college, reflected on the assault of positive accolades directed towards students during New Student Orientation: "Within 15 minutes, Morehouse College eliminated four years of negativity that my son experienced about himself in high school."[172]

While at Morehouse, students are inundated with positive superlatives about themselves and repeatedly told that as Morehouse students, they are "special," the "best of the best," and "the Talented Tenth." The extensive use of superlatives to enhance students' positive identity is unique to Morehouse College. The abundance of identifiable role models, many of whom are male and African American within the administration, faculty, staff, and alumni ranks help persuade students that they can achieve their goals. These

97

faculty and staff alums were themselves the beneficiaries of self-esteem building strategies during the administrations of former presidents as students, and they perpetuate the positive esteem building to current and future generations of students.

Giles states: "The legacy of Morehouse in developing positive contributors to their communities reveals a type of intellectual and cultural resistance to the entrenched negative stereotypes of Black men."[173] Historically, from the slavery era, African American men were considered lawless, hypersexual, and intellectually inferior. Today, they are projected by the media as thugs, criminals, and jocks.

Dr. Hope and Dr. Mays traditionally greeted students with, "Good Morning, Men of Morehouse," "Gentleman," or "Mister." These terms were used to strengthen the self-worth of students during pre-civil rights America when African American men were commonly belittled and called "nigger," "sambo," "rastus," "boy," and "uncle." While these overt references are rarely used today, African American males are still subjected to negative stereotypes and other social, racial, political, and economic factors that lessen their self-esteem. Morehouse attempts to counteract this negativity through positive messaging, and this is a consistent theme at New Student Orientation, convocations, Crown Forum, classroom lectures, and in printed materials. In addition, students are taught to be of good character, well-rounded, and community-minded.

To emphasize this point, Atlanta City Councilman H. Lamar Willis (class of 1993) recounted how the Dean of Admissions and Records, Sterling Hudson, explained the importance of esteem building at Morehouse during his prospective student interview. Dean Hudson told him: "We make sure that Morehouse Men walk out of here with an air

of confidence that's so high...they don't believe there is
anything insurmountable." Wills further recounted: "that was
one of the most interesting experiences that I had as a
student."[174]

Former CEO of Godfathers' Pizza, Herman Cain (class
of 1967) had a similar experience:

> "I believe the Morehouse experience impacted
> my leadership path in that I left there feeling
> that when given the opportunity to lead, I had
> to lead. It wasn't an option, I didn't have to go
> seek opportunity, opportunity just found me
> and I never hesitated to take on this project. It
> was because of the confidence that I gained
> while at Morehouse that caused me not to shy
> away from leadership opportunities."[175]

Morehouse reinforces positive self-image through the
use of verbal and non-verbal messages placed throughout the
campus in the form of slogans, quotes, historical portraits,
symbols, statues, and memorials that exalt Morehouse students
towards leadership. As current president Dr. Robert Michael
Franklin (class of 1975) observed, "...consider the message
of our landscape. The Morehouse campus is situated within
certain sacred landmarks that define our legacy and our
destiny."[176] Listed below are a few examples of this repetition
of messaging throughout the campus:

> "Some of the world's greatest leaders have entered
> through these doors."

Robert Hall Basement, Morehouse Post Office

"Whatever you do, strive to do it so well that no man living and no man dead, and no man yet to be born can do it any better. As we face the unpredictable future, have faith that man and God will assist us all the way."

Benjamin Elijah Mays National Memorial

"From Morehouse College he launched his humanitarian pilgrimage to create the beloved community, and for that purpose he moved out from the classroom and his pulpit to march his way into immortality."

Dr. Martin Luther King, Jr. Statue

As noted by Dr. Franklin during his 2007 Fall Convocation address, the campus monuments also are designed to transform the psyche of students:

"Everything we do on this campus happens between the pointing finger of Martin Luther King Jr. at one end of campus and the far-looking gaze of Mays at the other end of campus. Mays's gaze seems to invite us to focus on the purpose and destiny of Morehouse men. King's pointing finger seems to direct us toward the front lines of the social crisis where we are most needed. "But, look again, Mays appears to be peering out at President John Hope, who stands watch over the old front gate, warning all who enter here to abandon their egos. King stands tall, but he is flanked on one side by theologian and alumnus Howard Thurman who was Dr. King's chaplain at Boston University, and on the other side by Hugh Gloster, the architect of the modern Morehouse."[177]

Positive, repetitive messaging, both verbal and non-verbal, boosts the self-confidence of students. Supporting this point, University of Richmond law professor Benjamin Spencer (class of 1995) stated:

> "I grew in terms of my self-confidence and my aspirations. Morehouse forces you to think big, forces you to have high aspirations…at Morehouse, you're told: if you're going to go to law school, if you want to go to the best graduate school, if you're going to work on Wall Street, or if you want to go to the top places, we should try to be the best we can be. That's something I can point to Morehouse as the source of that drive within me and I know other people who went to Morehouse had that same drive. And it is reflected in the positions we hold now—all Morehouse alums end up excelling in whatever field they choose to enter."[178]

Rev. Calvin Butts (class of 1972), who maintains a dual professional role as the pastor of historic Abyssinian Baptist Church of Harlem and president of State University of New York at Westbrook, stated: "Morehouse instilled in me that sense that I could do anything in this world, in terms of professional work, integrity, and moral life. I can do anything. Yeah, sure, I can do anything, I'm a Morehouse Man."[179]

The Morehouse Mystique

A Bond of Brotherhood

Students are told as freshmen that they are being inaugurated into the Morehouse College Family. Within this family environment, students are challenged and nurtured by faculty and staff, but more importantly they are embraced by fellow African American students, an experience unparalleled for African American males by any other college or university within the United States.

Former Dean of Student Services Eddie Gaffney stated that the "biggest support to students is with each other." Gaffney stated that many African American parents want their sons to matriculate at Morehouse because it is the "best network for African American men in the country." These parents, according to Gaffney, "have seen how Morehouse Men operate and they want this for their sons. There is a synergy that is not in any other place. There is academic competition and students are reinforced by their peers."[180]

The expectation of brotherhood is specified in printed materials and supported by campus rituals. Brotherhood, a "unique camaraderie of spirit and purpose," begins while a student at Morehouse and continues as an alumnus. As the Admissions Viewbook explains to prospective students: "At Morehouse, you will experience the true meaning of brotherhood as you establish friendships with other students, who, like you, are on a journey to find their destinies."[181] It further states: "As an alumnus, you will belong to an amazing network of Morehouse graduates from all walks of life…. Whatever your need, there's sure to be a Morehouse brother just a phone call away."[182]

Most current students and alumni note that the Morehouse experience has helped them grow to understand

and appreciate their peers. Morehouse College, however, takes peer interactions to a higher level with its emphasis on brotherly ties. During Morehouse College's early days, the student body displayed an unusual amount of unity and harmony. Students referred to each other as "brothers." One of the school mottoes, "one for all and all for one," reinforced a spirit of oneness and brotherhood throughout the campus. In his autobiography, *With Head and Heart*, Dr. Howard Thurman (class of 1923) said that during the Hope presidential era, students ate together in the campus dining hall while the seniors sat together. According to Giles, "This process allowed for social reproduction of the Morehouse men, yet it promoted a deeper sense of belonging greater than the individual."[183]

Today, the college sanctions time-honored rituals to encourage the value of brotherhood. One such ritual is Spirit Night. Students bond with their peers, learn about the history of Morehouse, sing school-spirited songs, and hear expectations of student behavior from their elder brothers. Another is the singing of the College Hymn, "Dear Old Morehouse," which cultivates a spirit of brotherhood among students and alumni. The hymn, sung at convocations, athletics events, and all official functions of the college, is a sacred ritual revered by all. The song's lyrics speak to the loyalty that one has towards "Dear Old Morehouse," the brotherhood that students and alumni have towards each other, the strong character traits that Morehouse Men should strive to embody, and the recognition of the Supreme Being.

Morehouse also uses the Chapel experience (now Crown Forum) to promote brotherhood. Frank Peterman (class of 1985), a former member of the Florida House of Representatives and now Secretary of the Florida Department of Juvenile Justice, described one of his most cherished experiences of the Morehouse brotherhood:

> "I vividly remember one chapel service that had the greatest impression on me. The occasion was a Christmas assembly program in which the entire Morehouse student body of 1,900 Black men stood on their feet and sang "Faith of Our Fathers." Here was a rare sight of Black brothers who were not in jail or strung out on drugs, but singing a religious song. The sound was just mesmerizing. As we sang this song, I began to cry with joy and I covered my face so I wouldn't be noticed by the guys around me. It just broke me to see the brothers singing in one accord."[184]

Alumni reflect that the experience is akin to being in a fraternity. For example, Councilman Lamar Willis (class of 1993) stated:

> "I enrolled in Morehouse thinking it was going to be this wonderful all-male institution. The value I didn't expect, however, was going into an environment of all African American males and the magnitude of being in and around like-minded brothers who wanted positive things."[185]

Willis further added: "Morehouse is like a big fraternity. It doesn't matter if you're Omega, Kappa, Sigma, or Alpha…but Morehouse brothers just look out for everybody."[186]

Chapter 6: From Boys to Men – The Morehouse Mystique

Eddie Breaux (class of 2001), a former Peace Corps volunteer and current graduate student at Harvard University, stated,

> "...the brotherhood of Morehouse...was for me a very memorable experience. It is also like the larger fraternity, the brotherhood of Morehouse. The most memorable thing about my experience was the relationships, and the friendships that I made with people. There were students who were about business, students who were about success and making contributions to the world."[187]

Other thoughts about the brotherhood experience include the following:

> "...we learned at Morehouse there was something unique about a Morehouse Man that cannot be duplicated anywhere else. We were taught that when the chips are down and your back is against the wall, when the ceiling is caving in, and the floor is disintegrating, if there is a Morehouse Man anywhere in the area, he will pull you up."[188]

> Leroy Johnson (class of 1949)
> Former Georgia State Senator

> "I think I also learned how to have fun, enjoy life, and the camaraderie with my brothers. To this day, one of my best friends in the world is

somebody who was in my graduation class and several other people I was with in the Glee Club. Just the enjoyment of the fellowship was something I think was very critical and very important as a result of the Morehouse experience."[189]

> Herman Cain (class of 1967)
> CEO, *The Voice*, Atlanta, Georgia

"The most transforming experience of my life. And I really can't tell you what it meant to be on the campus with all those strong Black men, representing sort of a kind of challenge to academic excellence and integrity."[190]

> Dr. Calvin O. Butts (class of 1972)
> Pastor, Abyssinian Baptist Church, New York City
> President, SUNY at Westbrook

"...at a very early age, I had the experience of being able to talk with Morehouse Men that played sports in the community because they used to have all of their track meets and football games in the community and I was just very impressed with the spirit of the Morehouse students. That spirit is something that really dwelled within me...."[191]

> George Andrews (class of 1974)
> President & CEO, Capitol City Bank, Atlanta, Georgia

"The conversation that we had with guys was
one of the unique experiences, because we're
having these intellectual conversations with a
variety of black guys from all over the world,
getting different perspectives, and getting into
debates and things like that. That environment
you just can't duplicate. There's a teaching
environment that does not have a syllabus to
it, but it was the environment in the locker
room, and playing football with the guys."[192]

> Dr. Lloyd Edwards (class of 1980),
> Professor of Bio-statistics, School of
> Public Health, University of North
> Carolina, Chapel Hill, North Carolina

"I guess some of the best things about
Morehouse are things you don't realize or
understand until you leave. I've met brothers,
who you weren't tight with on campus, but
you understand...the value of the bond at
Morehouse, and so you look out for them as
alumni and try to do whatever you can for each
other."[193]

> Steve Crocker (class of 1983)
> Television news anchor, Birmingham,
> Alabama

"At Morehouse, you found folk who wanted
to be the best and brightest, wanted to do well,
wanted to excel and then also wanted to live

life to the fullest. And then for the first time in my life personally, I found like-minded individuals in such great numbers that it was a very supportive environment, different from what I had experienced growing up."[194]

H. Lamar Willis (class of 1993)
Councilman at Large; Atlanta, Georgia

The Modeling of the Morehouse Man

Modeling is defined by the On-line Dictionary for the Social Sciences as "a form of learning that occurs as a result of watching and imitating others." Merriam Webster's New Collegiate Dictionary also defines modeling as "to shape and form after a pattern."[195] Morehouse transforms its students through modeling and molding into distinctive prototypes, the Morehouse Men. These words describe the wide perception of how Morehouse College affects its students and makes them distinctive. This perception is held by people outside of the college as well as within. For example, there is a popular description about Morehouse students and alumni within the African American community: "You can always tell a Morehouse Man, but you can't tell him much." By the same token, Dr. Michael Lomax (class of 1968) described the importance of the Morehouse Man concept by stating:

"Dr. Benjamin Mays and other Morehouse administrators and faculty were saying, 'we are intentionally shaping you as men and future leaders. We not only expect you to meet an academic standard, but we expect you to meet

a social standard of how to dress, treat women,
and behave in society. Morehouse has branded
the Morehouse Man as one who is more than
a highly qualified professional, but a leader,
who is engaged in changing the world, and
forcing his personality, his values, and his
vision on the environment.'"[196]

Morehouse College, however, takes great pride in the
self-exaltation of the Morehouse Man. For example, former
president Dr. Walter Massey proclaimed to freshmen at the
1997 New Student Orientation:

"Morehouse Men are among the top in the
world. The Morehouse experience will be
rewarding. It will not be easy. It is not intended
to be easy. Our standards are high. We believe
that you can do it; otherwise, you would not
have been selected. You represent the best of
the best. You will be challenged to reach the
highest potential."[197]

Upon entering Morehouse as freshmen, students
undergo an extensive indoctrination about the responsibilities,
obligations, and expectations of what it means to become Men
of Morehouse that continues throughout their matriculation
at the institution. Upon the successful completion of their
studies as seniors, they are given the designation Morehouse
Men.

The Morehouse Man embodies all that is good, noble,
and strong in the African American educated male, possessing
the essential qualities of self-discipline, self-confidence, and

strength. The Admissions Viewbook quotes Nina Warfield (class of 1994), the college's first Rhodes Scholar: "I'm a Morehouse Man. Morehouse guided me, believed in me. Oxford University may be one of the best schools in the world, but it's Morehouse that got me here."[198]

By the same token, Morehouse students are expected to be well-rounded and to develop and foster spiritual and moral values. Dr. Robert Michael Franklin, in his 2008 Presidential Charge to graduating seniors, said that Morehouse Men should be "well read, well traveled, well spoken, well dressed, and well balanced in life."[199] Similarly, the Admissions Viewbook states that Morehouse expects its students to be "outstanding men and extraordinary leaders to serve God and humanity."[200]

Councilman H. Lamar Willis (class of 1993) stated: "My first real taste of how I should present myself as a man, how I should dress, and how I should talk…I learned when I got to Morehouse."[201] Councilman Willis further stated:

> "I think the most interesting thing I took away from my Morehouse experience was presentation. Morehouse taught students how to present themselves from the very beginning until the very end. From making sure students were dressed right, that they should look folk in the eye while shaking another person's hand, and that students had to display proper etiquette if they went to dinner…those are the things I took away from my Morehouse experience."[202]

Chapter 6: From Boys to Men – The Morehouse Mystique

Anthony Harris, current opinions editor of the Maroon Tiger, asked the rhetorical question, "What is a Morehouse Man?"

"The new Morehouse Man is a synthesis of all our greatest attributes. ...he is the DuBois and the Washington. He is Paul the Apostle, all things to all people. He is a beacon to the world of what the Black man can be: anything.

This is not to say that he is capable of being a CEO of a Fortune 500 company, although he is. It says he can be one of the few Black men working as schoolteachers, despite how little money they earn. It says he can rap the truth on the radio... (and) It says he can run a nice restaurant on Peachtree Street.

The greatness of the Morehouse Man will continue to shine, but we should not be discouraged if the light is not the same. Just as language, society and music changes so must we. Our standards for one another must change. Our standards for Morehouse must change. We shall continue to strive for excellence, but we must also recognize what excellence is in the 21st century.
A Morehouse Man is what we shall be some day, and it shall be the greatness that we aspire to be, in all shapes and forms."[203]

In sum, the personification of the ideals and values of Morehouse College is the Morehouse Man. Addie Butler in her book, *The Distinctive College: Talladega, Tuskegee, and Morehouse* described the Morehouse Man as a "unique being" that Morehouse College produces of "consistently high caliber."[204] The Morehouse Man possesses:

> "a great love for his alma mater...a strong loyalty to his fellow alumni...a great appreciation for the fairer sex...an unusual talent for public speaking...a keen appreciation for academic achievement...a strong desire for professional success...a deep commitment to racial progress...and an unusual initiative in his various undertakings."[205]

A Climate of Celebration

According to Peterson and Deal, "Recognition ceremonies pay tribute to the special accomplishments of individuals and groups thereby forging pride and respect."[206] Morehouse College places a high premium on celebrating the well deserved accomplishments of students and alumni through time-honored traditions, rituals, and ceremonies. Among the campus sanctioned ceremonies is Scholars' Day (formerly Honors' Day). This annual event pays tribute to students who have performed exemplary in the classroom as well as displayed consummate leadership on campus and in the community. Scholars' Day is an opportunity for the college to applaud academic excellence, which is a rare occurrence for African American males in higher education. Without mentioning or imaging athletics, Scholars' Day is akin to an

academic pep rally, where young African American men are
lauded, congratulated, and applauded for their academic
achievements in the classroom as well as exemplary acts of
service in the community.
Many top officials, such as the president and provost,
participate in this event. This communicates a powerful
affirmation of the college's commitment to academic
excellence. Scholars' Day is an all-campus assembly and even
non-recognized students join in the celebration of lauding the
accomplishments of their peers.

Another campus-sanctioned celebration is
Commencement, the culmination of four years of hard work
and of meeting the college's graduation standards. This annual
ceremony is truly a celebratory occasion for students and their
families, faculty and staff, special guests, and alumni from
various reunion classes who eagerly wait to welcome their
new crop of brothers. The presence of African drummers at
the head of the graduation processional signals that this is a
festive occasion. The commencement program is meticulously
choreographed, and the event ends with the singing of Dear
Old Morehouse, followed by a benediction.

Commencement is the final step in the rites-of-passage
progression of rituals. Educators and social scientists often
refer to this as the "incorporation" stage in which participants
are formally admitted into new roles.[207] Graduating seniors
are given their final challenge before being anointed as
Morehouse Men. The climatic moment is the receipt of the
diplomas, followed by the "turning of the tassel" ceremony
(presided over by the provost and the departmental deans),
induction into the Morehouse alumni association by the
National Alumni President who welcomes graduates into the
"brotherhood of Morehouse Men," and the proclamation by

113

the college president that the graduates are now official Morehouse Men.

Consistent with many of the other campus-wide assemblies, graduating seniors are frequently referred to by such superlatives as "best," "excellent," and "outstanding." In his 1998 President's Charge, Dr. Walter Massey lauded the graduates for their accomplishments and told them that they were special, and they were expected to embody these qualities as alumni. Dr. Robert Michael Franklin's 2008 President's Charge succinctly challenged graduates to "go forth and lead" and become "well read, well traveled, well spoken, well dressed, and well balanced in life."[208]

Chapter 7: Morehouse College Today

"We learned on the first day that we walked on this campus, that this (Morehouse) is a holy place."[209]

Dr. Lerone Bennett, Jr. (class of 1949)
Morehouse College Trustee and Former Executive Editor,
Ebony Magazine

By the end of the Mays era in 1967, Morehouse College had grown substantially in faculty, student enrollment, endowment, and international reputation. Today, 10 academic buildings, 12 residence halls, a presidential residence, student life facilities, and athletic facilities sit on 61 acres.

Campus buildings symbolize in brick and mortar the institution's core values, and they memorialize the men who played important roles not only in the history of Morehouse but Black America as well. Buildings such as Graves, Robert, Sale, Hope, Mays, and Dansby are named in honor of the college's founding fathers, past presidents, distinguished faculty, and prominent alumni. Other buildings, such as DuBois, Danforth, and Douglass, bear the name of prominent African American men of history and white benefactors of the college.

Even the post office instills a sense of pride. One of the most visited buildings on campus, the post office is located in the basement of the Robert Hall dormitory. Inside the hallway a sign reads, "Some of the world's greatest leaders have entered through these doors."

The campus serves as the final resting place of former Morehouse presidents Hope, Mays (and his second wife, Sadie Gray Mays), and Gloster. These graves serve as an everyday reminder of the role these men played in the development of the college. Students and alumni pay homage to these former college leaders during special ceremonies, such as Founders' Day and Commencement. Alumni who were mentored and "fathered" by Dr. Mays can at times be seen bending their knees to pray at his crypt.

As previously mentioned, the most prominent building on campus is the Martin Luther King, Jr. International Chapel. Built in 1978, its purpose is to teach excellence, ethics, equality, and engagement.

Inside King Chapel, quotes from Dr. King's speeches are inscribed on the walls in the lobby. Life-sized portraits of prominent Africans and African Americans in business, education, entertainment, and civil rights are showcased in the Hall of Honor. Leaders include former South African President Nelson Mandela, Afrocentrist historian Dr. Cheikh Anta Diop, civil rights veterans Rev. Jesse Jackson and Rev. Joseph Lowery, soloist and human rights activist Paul Robeson, and former United Nations Ambassador Rev. Andrew Young. Also displayed are portraits of notable women, including Coretta Scott King and Harriet Tubman.

Adjacent to King Chapel is Gloster Hall, named in honor of Dr. Hugh Gloster, the college's seventh president. Gloster Hall houses most of the administrative offices, including the Office of the President, the Senior Vice President for Academic Affairs, Business and Finance, and the Admissions Office.

The Howard Washington Thurman Memorial, named for the distinguished Morehouse alumnus, sits next to King Chapel. Inscribed on the base of the memorial is Thurman's famous quote: "Over the heads of her students Morehouse holds a crown that she challenges them to grow tall enough to wear."

The athletic facilities may be modest, but they are notable. They bear the names of distinguished scholar athletes and coaches. The football stadium (seats 9,000) is named in honor of Burwell T. Harvey, a physics and chemistry instructor at Morehouse and one of the college's most successful coaches. The basketball arena (seats 5,500) was named for Dr. Franklin Forbes (class of 1923) and was built for the 1996 Atlanta Olympic Games. In addition, there are tennis courts, an Olympic size swimming pool, and a track named in honor of U.S. Olympian Edwin Moses (class of 1978). Morehouse is a member of the Southern Intercollegiate Athletic Conference (SIAC) and the National Collegiate Athletic Association (NCAA), Division II. Varsity letter sports include football, basketball, tennis, cross country, and track and field.

Campus buildings, however, tell only part of the Morehouse story. The college has evolved into a Mecca for young Black men. Its single-gender and cultural environment offer a rich tradition, a challenging and nurturing orientation, visible role models, and an environment free of racism.

Seventy-one percent of students say that Morehouse was their first choice, with the school's reputation for producing leaders being the deciding factor.[210] The opening sentence of the *Admissions Viewbook* states:

> "When you step onto the campus of Morehouse College…you immediately are aware of both your history and your destiny. Morehouse's history is so impressive, so tangible, that you can't help but be filled with a keen sense of awe and respect for the men

who have come to this place before you and gone on to make outstanding contributions to society." [211]

The Classroom Experience

The average class size at Morehouse is small. This creates a sense of intimacy and encourages close interaction between faculty and students. I observed the interrelationship between students and faculty during a core history class. I wanted to understand how an advantageous teacher-student ratio impacted students' aspirations for leadership and scholarship.

Observations

On April 30, 1998, I was invited by Herman Mason, assistant history professor, to observe his final spring semester class of 30 freshmen and sophomores. The class was held in Brawley Hall, room 100.

Arriving at about 10:55 a.m., I sat in the back of the classroom so that I could observe students and teacher with minimum distractions. As the students arrived, Professor Mason greeted each student and had informal conversations with some. Formal instruction commenced at approximately 11:10 a.m. Mason addressed each student as "Mister." If a student was asked to speak, he had to stand and then give his answer.

An introduction to history, this course was required of all students. During this particular class session, the professor presented a chronological review of U.S. presidents. The lecture was designed to assess the note-taking capability of students in their preparation for the final examination and to review topics that had been discussed in previous lectures, including the Dred Scott decision, the John Brown "Harper's Ferry" uprising, and the relationship of these events to American slavery. Also discussed was the difference between abolitionists and non-abolitionists. Mason taught history from an African American perspective. He presented a more enlightened view of Lincoln and his true views on slavery, the Emancipation Proclamation, the Freedman's Bureau, and the effect of the Civil War on the nation. The classroom session ended at 12:00 p.m.

Learning history from such a fresh perspective might have shaken the world view of some students, but that is what Morehouse is all about. Professor Mason encouraged participation by frequently calling upon students to respond to questions. Public speaking and critical thinking skills were being honed. The tradition of students raising their hands and standing to answer questions instills respect for the process, the teacher, and fellow students. It says that education is important.

Professor Mason treated his students with dignity by addressing them by their surnames. Although his questions were challenging, he clearly respected their intelligence.

I thoroughly enjoyed observing this history class. The professor had a good command of his class. The students were attentive, participated enthusiastically, seemed excited to learn, were manly and mannerly, responded well to the professor, and demonstrated respect for the professor and the course material.

Interactions between the African American male professor and students are rare in today's society. It is conceivable that African American males will go through their entire school career, from kindergarten to college, and not have an African American male teacher. In an age when academic success is devalued by some African American males because it is perceived as "acting white" or "selling out."[212] It was quite refreshing to observe African American male students genuinely interested in learning.

Events and Ceremonies

According to Deal and Peterson, "Most schools have some formal ceremonies... (that) are complex, culturally sanctioned ways that a school celebrates successes, communicates values, and recognizes special contributions of staff and students."[213] This is definitely the case with Morehouse. During the course of the academic year, several time-honored traditions reinforce the college's mission. These events and ceremonies include New Student Orientation, Fall Opening Convocation, Founders' Day Convocation, Scholars' Convocation, Baccalaureate, and Commencement. Each event honors the school's history, possesses strong symbolism, and reinvigorates the values of the college.

New Student Orientation. As early as the 1930s, the college provided a three-day program to immerse new students into the campus culture, introduce them to faculty, and acquaint them with the academic programs. By the 1960s, as student enrollment increased, the three-day program evolved into "Freshman Week."

Today, Morehouse provides an eight-day orientation program. Based on the traditions of the past, the program is a rites-of-passage journey. The elders of the academic community receive their sons in embryonic states and provide them with an intensive four-year incubation period of teaching, challenging, mentoring, cajoling, and celebrating, thus facilitating students' maturation into higher levels of manhood.

Social scientists would call New Student Orientation the "separation stage" in the journey to manhood. This first round of activities provides a deliberate break from students' identification with high school by introducing them to campus life, academic programs, school policies, and Morehouse traditions. Upperclassmen play a large role in the planning and execution of New Student Orientation, and a senior year student serves as director.

New Student Orientation begins the process of transformation from boys to men, students to scholars. It is a literal wake up call for incoming students. With the traditional "ringing of the bell" ceremony near Robert Hall, upper classmen lecture freshmen about their new identity as Men of Morehouse and the expectations the school has of them.

In the "look to your left and look to your right" ritual, students are asked to look at their brothers seated next to them. They are then challenged to avoid the distractions that lead to dropping out and failure. According to the former Director of Off-Campus Student Affairs, J. Stacy Grayson (class of 1983), this ritual is highly effective:

> "…it all begins those first few days when you come here and you really start having to take a look at yourself and say this is who I am and this is what I have to do. It is a wake up experience….To see a mirror image of yourself in other people who are doing well, excelling, and exceeding and striving." [214]

121

Spirit Night. One of the long-standing traditions of New Student Orientation is Spirit Night. Student leaders are in charge of this officially sanctioned activity. Freshmen are awakened at 5:00 a.m. by their "elder brothers," paraded across campus in single file lines, taught Morehouse school songs, schooled on the importance of brotherhood, and challenged to uphold the tradition of excellence.

Students are taken to three historic campus monuments to receive their charge as Men of Morehouse. At the foot of the King statue, students are challenged, in the spirit of one of King's last sermons, to "stay awake." Next, they go to the Thurman Memorial where they hear his mantra, "Over the heads of her students Morehouse holds a crown that she challenges them to grow tall enough to wear." Students then go to the Mays Memorial site, where they hear Mays' eternal edict, **"Whatever you do, strive to do it so well that no man living and no man dead, and no man yet to be born can do it any better."** This peer-led ritual is passed on in an oral tradition, "mouth to ear," and is a powerful initiator into the brotherhood, culture, and expectations of Morehouse.

John Wilson, a current student from Bessemer City, North Carolina, says that "Talking and singing the school hymn with my brothers at 5 o'clock in the morning is rough. This morning we were fed the rich history of Morehouse by upperclassmen. They want us to be sure we know where we are so that we may carry ourselves accordingly."[215] Benjamin Spencer (class of 1995), a law professor at the University of Richmond, remembers his initiation into Morehouse:

"The first most memorable experience dates back to the first week of my time at Morehouse. That's the Freshman Week experience, which at the time culminated into Spirit Night. It was an event where the freshman class was led around the local community, and we ended up in a tent in the middle of the night. Learning, hearing different stories from upper classmen and learning different songs and really developing a strong bond as men of Morehouse. So, Spirit Night was really a wonderful kind of rite-of-passage that made us all transformed from high school students into men of Morehouse. It had a real bond. That was a very valuable, early experience in my Morehouse career."[216]

New Student Convocation. Among the many orientation activities, the New Student Convocation is the most significant. This ceremony is the administration's official "welcome" of new students into the Morehouse College family.

I attended the New Student Convocation on August 18, 1997, at King Chapel. Alvin Darden (class of 1972), Dean of the Freshman Class, presided over the program. The Convocation was attended by first year students, new transfer students, top-level administrators, faculty, and staff.

Observations

I arrived at the 2,000-seat Martin Luther King, Jr. Chapel at 8:30 a.m. The hall was empty. I sat on the first row, left side of the stage so that I could observe students as they entered the building. At 8:50 a.m., approximately 800

The Morehouse Mystique

Morehouse first-year and transfer students began filing into King Chapel. Students were escorted to their seats by approximately 25 Student Orientation Leaders. All students were handsomely attired and wore a shirt and tie. They were mannerly and quiet as they sat in their seats.

Then the administrators filed into the hall. Nearly all top administrators are Morehouse graduates. They entered from the right side of the stage and walked in single file to their seats, which were lined across the stage behind the podium. What an impressive array of distinguished men and women! All were dressed in business suits. Dean Darden opened the session at 9:00 a.m. Following his remarks was a musical interlude on the pipe organ by Dr. David Morrow (class of 1980). The music was solemn but soothing.

Dr. Lawrence Carter, Dean of King Chapel, then approached the podium. In a stern voice Dr. Carter said, "To the historic class of 2001, according to Aristotle, 'The brave are found where bravery is honored' and according to Martin L. King, 'My success depends on you.'" He then gave the invocation.

Dean Darden explained the purpose of the ceremony as an opportunity for students to meet the executive officers of the college and to put names with faces. Most importantly, they were now officially inaugurated into the Morehouse family.

Dr. Uzze Brown (class of 1972), a professor in the music department, sang "Hold On," the African American spiritual, in a deep, baritone voice. There is a verse that goes, "If dat plow stays in yo' hand, it'll lan' you straight into de promised lan'..." The song teaches the value of persistence, dedication, and perseverance. It was a powerful message to students.

Next Dr. Anne Watts, Vice Provost for Academic Programs, introduced the guests on the platform. She proclaimed, "Greatness is predictable for those who are uncomfortable with mediocrity."

Provost Dr. John Hopps (class of 1958) welcomed students to "the House." He told the students,

"You are above average in character. You are the best. I expect to see you four years from now in line for graduation to obtain your baccalaureate degree. Academic excellence has been the hallmark at Morehouse College. Nearly all faculty members have a doctorate or terminal degree in their major field. You should use every opportunity to get to know the institution and what it means to be a Morehouse Man."

President Dr. Walter Massey (class of 1958) said,

"You are joining a community, a team, a family. We believe that every group of entering freshmen is special. Graduates of this class will be the first graduates of the new millennium. You should work together and in partnership. You will have a variety of experiences. Academics are first and foremost, but also learn ethical and moral principles.

"The primary mission of Morehouse College is to educate African American men. Morehouse Men are among the top in the world. The Morehouse experience will be rewarding. It will not be easy. It is not intended to be easy. Our standards are high. We believe that you can do it; otherwise you would not have been selected. You represent the best of the best. You will be challenged to reach your highest potential.

"It is the responsibility of all to make Morehouse the best house. The Morehouse mascot is 'Tiger Smart,' which [represents being] studious, mature, ambitious, resourceful, and tenacious. Are you Tiger Smart? Over the next four years, you will transition from being Men of Morehouse to Morehouse Men."

Students so enjoyed Dr. Massey's speech that they gave him a standing ovation. Finally, Dean Darden gave the closing remarks. We then rose to our feet, linked arms, and sang the College Hymn, "Dear Old Morehouse."
Colleges that do an effective job of engaging students employ an "ethic of membership."[217] They are committed to doing everything they can to help students succeed.

The ethic of membership clearly drives the Morehouse mission, and as I sat in that great hall, I was fully persuaded that the administration and faculty were committed to students' success. Surely students appreciated just how special and blessed they were to have been accepted by Morehouse. That day they became members of the Morehouse family. The next four years would not be easy, but with the supportive environment of Morehouse, I felt confident they would rise to the challenge.

Fall Opening Convocation. Three of the most important ceremonies of the academic year at Morehouse College are Fall Convocation, Founders Day Convocation, and Commencement. Symbolizing the importance of these ceremonies, senior level administrators and faculty attend the proceedings robed in full academic regalia. Alumni and special guests of the college are invited to attend. In the Fall Convocation, the senior academic officer presides, but the highlight of the program is the address given by the college president.

On September 18, 1997, I attended the Opening Convocation held at King Chapel. This ceremony serves as the official kick-off event for the academic school year. Student attendance was mandatory, and most faculty, staff, and employees of the college attended as well. Seating was filled to capacity. The impressive ceremony was solemn, yet festive.

Observations

I arrived at King Chapel at 10:45 a.m. and sat on the right side, near the front. At 10:50 a.m., the Convocation began with the procession of faculty, who entered the hall down the center aisle. Dr. Tobe Johnson (class of 1954), Chair of the Political Science Department and one of the most senior staff, led the faculty. Then the seniors, dressed in shirt and tie, walked in, followed by the platform guests. President Massey, adorned in a maroon and white academic robe, came in last.

Dr. Hopps called the Convocation to order and declared "the academic year in full session." After Dr. Carter gave the opening prayer, Dr. Hopps spoke of the significance of the occasion. He said the Convocation was "intended to espouse excellence in a formal setting and to reinforce educational excellence." He said that students should pledge excellence throughout the academic year and that they were required to dress in shirt and tie as a symbol of giving and doing their best.

The main highlight of the Convocation was the address by President Massey entitled, "Let us now praise famous men."

"All people are given by the Divine the potential for excellence. Excellence is attainable. Morehouse has trained men for leadership by nurturing and challenging. Some of the most famous men in the world are Morehouse graduates, such as Martin Luther King, Maynard Jackson, Edwin Moses, and Dr. David Satcher. All these men came to Morehouse with unrealized potential. They took advantage of the offerings at Morehouse. You can be famous men. Look around you, behind you. These Morehouse brothers are tomorrow's lawyers, politicians, and engineers.

Remember to respect each other, praise, affirm each other, because one day you will be famous..."

Dr. Massey's speech had a tremendous effect on the students. He told them they were special and had the potential to be famous—and I think those young men believed him. I can imagine that all doubts about their ability to meet the academic challenges of the coming year dissolved in the grace and power of his words. He offered students the gift of a brilliant future, as long as they stayed the course, maintained discipline, and did their best.

The presidential address touched the hearts and minds of the entire Morehouse College family. The message reaffirmed the mission of the college, namely, leadership development. The administration, faculty, and staff were given their charge to develop Morehouse students into leaders.

We gave President Massey a thunderous ovation. Then SGA President William Sellers shared a "meditation moment," and the Glee Club sang "Get on Board." The Convocation officially ended at 12:30 p.m. with all in attendance rising to their feet to sing the College Hymn, "Dear Old Morehouse."

Founders' Day Convocation. Founders' Convocation is held in February. This ceremony honors the men who were instrumental in the establishment of Morehouse College. Traditionally, the celebration features a prominent Morehouse alumnus as the keynote speaker. Student attendance is mandatory, and faculty, staff, and alumni attend as well.

Observations

I attended the Founders' Day Convocation at Morehouse College on February 12, 1998. The Convocation was held at King Chapel. The purpose of the Convocation was to celebrate the 131st anniversary of the founding of Morehouse College.

I arrived at King Chapel just before the program began. The Chapel was nearly filled to capacity. The Convocation began at 10:45 a.m. with the processional of faculty, who were attired in their academic regalia. Dr. Massey and the keynote speaker, Mr. Herman Cain (class of 1967), followed. We prayed and then sang "Lift Every Voice and Sing," the Black National Anthem.

Dr. Massey, in his opening remarks, explained that the purpose of Founders' Day was to "celebrate the past, reflect on the present, and ponder the future." He referred to the accomplishments of Morehouse alumni, including the recent appointment and confirmation of Dr. David Satcher (class of 1963) as the Surgeon General of the United States. Dr. Massey said that "Morehouse still is making a positive difference in the world" and that "producing leaders is Morehouse's legacy."

The highlight of the program was the keynote address given by Mr. Cain, who currently serves as CEO of the National Restaurant Association and former CEO of Godfathers' Pizza. A classic "rags to riches" story, students had the privilege of hearing one example of how a Morehouse Man's self-esteem is built.

Mr. Cain described himself as an average person when he came to Morehouse, but he left as a leader ready to take on the world. His message to students was that despite life's circumstances, "You can do it too!" After the speech, the Glee Club sang "A New Heart Will I Give You."

The Convocation concluded with the conferring of honorary degrees to Joseph and Emma Adams. Their significant financial contributions to Morehouse endowed community service scholarships. Presidential Awards of Distinction were presented to Dr. James Ellison (class of 1938), college physician for more than 40 years, and Ms. Ingrid Saunders Jones, Vice President of Corporate External Affairs for the Coca Cola Foundation, a benefactor of the college. The convocation ended at 12:45 p.m. with students linking arms and singing the College Hymn, "Dear Old Morehouse."

Numerous studies have found that Black colleges excel at fostering educational success among African American students. For example, educational researchers George Kuh and Lemuel Watson found that the Black college environment, which emphasizes the development of academic, scholarly, and intellectual abilities, appears to be the most influential factor in students' educational gains.[218] Patricia Gurin and Edgar Epps found that African American students who attend Black colleges possessed a positive self-image, strong racial pride, and high aspirations.[219]

As I listened to Dr. Massey and Mr. Cain, I realized that by honoring famous Morehouse alumni and challenging students to follow in their footsteps, this Convocation was developing pride, self-worth, and a strong identity. It is certainly the case with my fellow alumni that I have known over the years. What distinguishes the Morehouse Man is the high self-esteem we enjoy.

Scholar's Day Assembly. The Scholars' Day program began in the 1920's as the bi-annual Honors' Day program. Students who maintained a B average or above and who had no lower than a C in any subject were recognized. This tradition of honoring academic excellence continues today. The purpose of the Scholars' Day program is to recognize academic achievers who made the honor role or dean's list and who were accepted into Phi Beta Kappa or other academic honor societies.

Observations

I attended the Scholars' Day program on April 23, 1998. The program theme was "A Celebration of Excellence," and it was held at King Chapel. Student attendance was mandatory. Also in attendance were Dr. Massey, Dr. Hopps, and faculty and staff.

The Occasion was given by Dr. Anne Watts, who challenged the students by stating: "Making the honor roll is not an easy task at Morehouse. Many of you have the ability to be on the Honor Roll. I challenge you!"

All students on the Honor Roll and Dean's List were asked to stand. Seven Morehouse students with a cumulative GPA of 4.0 received a plaque and were congratulated by President Massey and Provost Hopps.

Recognition then went to students who participated in various academic honor societies and service programs, including Americorps Scholars, Alpha Epsilon Delta (pre-medical students), the Phi Chi National Honor Society (psychology students), the Bonners Scholars Program (service learning students), the Dansby Scholars (math students), the Merrill Scholars (study abroad students), and Sigma Tau Delta (English students).

As I observed the ceremony I wondered how many other colleges and universities could boast such a proud occasion of honoring so many Black men. Not many, I guessed. This was indeed a rare occasion, and I couldn't escape the feeling that history was in the making. How could honor students not receive a boost to their self-esteem as they were applauded by their peers? This program was more like a pep rally, only for academic success. African American young men were lauded, congratulated, and applauded for their achievements in the classroom—what an awesome sight!

Baccalaureate. Baccalaureate is a tradition that has been observed at Morehouse College for many years.

Chapter 7: Morehouse College Today

Essentially a religious service, Baccalaureate is held on the Saturday preceding the Sunday Commencement. Baccalaureate consists of greetings by college officials, songs by the Morehouse Glee Club, a scripture reading, a sermon by a distinguished minister, and a benediction.

Observation

On May 16, 1998, I attended the Baccalaureate service at Morehouse College, which was held in King Chapel. There was standing room only. Attendees included graduating seniors, faculty, staff, parents, guests, and Morehouse alumni.

When I arrived at around 2:30 p.m., I was greeted by a buzz of energy, excitement, and anticipation. At 2:43 p.m., Dr. Tobe Johnson (class of 1954), the Mace-bearer and Chief Faculty Marshal, entered with the Mace. According to Dr. Johnson, the Mace symbolizes the authority of the college. One of the mottos of the college, *Et Facta Est Lux* ("And there was light"), is inscribed in Latin on the Mace.

The senior class of 1998, all wearing black graduation robes and caps, entered at 2:45 p.m. This was a proud moment for family members, especially parents, who applauded and cheered loudly as their sons entered the Chapel to take their seats.

The processional also consisted of the faculty and platform guests, who followed the seniors into the Chapel. President Massey brought up the rear of the processional. There were approximately 20 platform guests, including the college President, Provost, senior-level vice presidents, the Dean of King Chapel, the Chairman of the Board of Trustees, and the Baccalaureate speaker. Faculty, platform guests, and graduating seniors were attired in full academic regalia.

133

After the prelude and processional, the program officially began at 3:00 p.m. with "The Occasion" given by Dr. Otis Moss, Jr. (class of 1956), Chairman of the Board of Trustees. Dr. Moss, pastor of Olivet Institutional Baptist Church in Cleveland, Ohio, is considered one of America's greatest Black preachers. He spoke eloquently about the spiritual audacity of Morehouse. He challenged the graduates to "lift up Morehouse" and "carry your load to help others bear their burden." He also spoke of moral integrity. He concluded by saying, "We expect Morehouse, through you, to succeed."

The Glee Club, under the direction of Dr. Morrow, sang "Our God Our Help in Ages Past." Psalm 139 was read by the senior class president, Albert Lee Miller.

Dr. Massey introduced the speaker, Dr. Robert Michael Franklin (class of 1975), President, Interdenominational Theological Center (and appointed President of Morehouse College on July 1, 2007). He delivered one of the most dynamic sermons I have ever heard. With tremendous eloquence, Dr. Franklin talked about the plight of the Black male in today's society, and the audience responded with shouts of "Amen!" He challenged the graduates to do what they could to help the community. He said, quoting Luke 12:48, "To whom much is given much is required." He said the graduates should be honored for their achievement. Dr. Franklin ended his speech to a thunderous standing ovation with the graduating seniors enthusiastically leaping to their feet.

Following the Baccalaureate address, two individuals were honored by Morehouse for their lifetime achievements. Their portraits hung in the Morehouse College Hall of Fame, which houses the portraits of many distinguished Morehouse alumni.

One of the honorees was Atlanta Mayor Maynard Jackson. He said, "Morehouse is the greatest college in this country! If you don't use your power to make a difference, you don't need power." He challenged the grads to do everything within their power to eliminate racism.

The second honoree was Mrs. Coretta Scott King, wife of Dr. Martin Luther King, Jr. She joked, "You can always tell a Morehouse Man, but you can't tell him much." Seriously she said, "You're going to make a difference." The program ended at 5:00 p.m. with a recessional by the graduates, platform guests, and faculty.

Baccalaureate was truly a moving experience. The electricity in the air at the beginning of the program rose to a feverish pitch during Dr. Franklin's sermon. The event was a proud moment for family, especially parents. Students were commended for the accomplishment of graduating from Morehouse, and they were challenged to continue along the path of excellence as they went out into the world.

Commencement. The final official event of the academic year was the 114th Commencement, held on May 17, 1998. This Commencement was noteworthy for the college. It marked the 50th anniversary of the graduation of Dr. Martin Luther King, Jr. and the 75th anniversary of Dr. Howard Thurman's graduation. Commencement was held outside on the grounds of the old campus between Graves Hall and Harkness Hall.

The Commencement program started at 8:00 a.m. on a hot, humid Sunday morning. Approximately 10,000 family, friends, well-wishers, and alumni were present. President Massey presided over the ceremony.

Like the Baccalaureate service on the previous day, there was a buzz of excitement before the program officially began. Dr. Anne Watts opened the event with the "Call to Order and the Crowning Moment." The processional was led by a troupe of African drummers, who enthusiastically set the tone as a celebratory event. The drummers were followed by the faculty, platform guests, and graduating seniors, who were arrayed in their colorful academic regalia.

Next there was the traditional "ringing of the bell," a ritual that harkened back to the first bell that was housed at Springfield Baptist Church (the founding site of Morehouse College) in Augusta, Georgia. We sang "Lift Every Voice and Sing," then Dean Lawrence Carter prayed.

Dr. Massey gave his greetings. His most notable comment was, "You are no longer Men of Morehouse. You now have the privilege of being called Morehouse Men." The Honorable Willie Brown, mayor of San Francisco, then challenged the graduates to make the world a better place.

After the conferring of degrees, Dr. Massey gave the traditional "Charge to the Graduates." He said, "You deserve to be proud of your accomplishments today. By earning your baccalaureate degree, you have done what few other African American men your age have done. You are special in that regard." Dr. Massey cautioned the graduates not to rest on their laurels. He said,

"To whom much is given, *more* is required. You entered Morehouse to learn, you depart to serve. That is what a Morehouse education is all about—gaining much in terms of knowledge and skills and values—so that you may give much in terms of contributions to the world...I charge you to go forth and serve—serve your families, your community, your alma mater, your nation, and your God."[220]

Distinguished alumni, including Spike Lee and Lerone Bennett, Jr., were in attendance. Speaker after speaker lavished inspiration and praise upon the graduates. They were told they were "the best," "excellent," and "outstanding."

Chapter 8: Perspectives of Presidents, Faculty, and Staff

"My vision for Morehouse College is that it will be among the very finest private, undergraduate liberal arts colleges in the world."[221]

Dr. Walter E. Massey
President, Morehouse College

Throughout its history, Morehouse College has been privileged to have had strong, visionary, presidential leadership. The President has the administrative function of providing day-to-day oversight of the college and raising funds. He also performs a ceremonial function by serving as the head of the institution, officiating over convocations and ceremonies, and articulating the vision of the college.

Dr. Walter E. Massey

Dr. Walter Eugene Massey became the ninth President of Morehouse on June 1, 1995, and fulfilled his presidential role with distinction until his retirement on June 30, 2007. Prior to becoming President, Massey was Provost and Senior Vice President of the University of California System (a post he created at Morehouse). A noted physicist, he was the former Director of the National Science Foundation.

After obtaining his Bachelor of Science degree in physics from Morehouse College in 1958, Massey earned his Master of Science and Ph.D. in physics from Washington University in 1966. He served as a professor of physics and Dean of the college at Brown University. Later, he was named

Vice President for Research and Director of the prestigious Argonne Laboratory at the University of Chicago. In 1991, President George H. Bush appointed Dr. Massey to serve as Director of the National Science Foundation.

Dr. Walter E. Massey

As President, Dr. Massey called on the Morehouse community to renew its longstanding commitment to excellence in scholarship. Under his leadership, the college embraced the challenge of preparing for the 21st century and the goal of becoming one of the nation's best liberal arts colleges. In Massey's words:

> "The universe of institutions against which we measure our progress and standards must encompass all of the finest colleges and universities, not just those with origins similar to our own. All the while, we will continue to be an institution that focuses on the development of leaders and the college of choice for African American men."[222]

Under Massey's presidency, Morehouse expanded its dual-degree master's program in natural sciences with the Georgia Institute of Technology to include other institutions and social science majors. He launched the Center for Excellence in Science, Engineering and Mathematics with a $6.7 million grant from the U.S. Department of Defense. A new African American Studies program was established. The Department of Economics and Business Administration earned accreditation from the American Association of Schools and Colleges of Business (AASCB), resulting in Morehouse becoming one of only a handful of liberal arts colleges in the country that has both AASCB accreditation and a Phi Beta Kappa chapter. The college also renewed its accreditation from the Southern Association of Colleges and Schools.

In his inaugural speech on February 16, 1996, President Massey described his vision of Morehouse as a world-class institution.

"Historically, Morehouse has focused its preparation of students primarily on building leaders for community and national roles. But today, we must expand our mission to produce leaders also for the global metropolis that the world will be in the next century."

He further stated:

"Creating an educational experience that cultivates these characteristics (self-confidence, self-worth, and self-identity) in our students is something Morehouse has done exceptionally well for more than a century. And we will continue that tradition as a strong, undergraduate, liberal arts institution with a focus on producing outstanding leaders.

But today, we must expand our mission to ensure that our students are prepared to assume leadership roles not only in a more diverse America—but in the steadily shrinking world we share. We will prepare our students for the new global metropolis by drawing on the strengths of our past to cultivate within ourselves and our students an intellectual confidence and curiosity that will equip us for lifelong learning and growth."

President Massey concluded with a challenge to faculty and staff:

"Above all, we will prepare our students by continuing to engage them in an intellectual, moral and ethical dialogue that underscores our recommitment to a culture of excellence, a dialogue that will take place not only in classrooms, but wherever we interact—in hallways, dormitories and dining rooms, on athletic fields, and in offices and chapels.

Indeed, our goal is nothing less than excellence in every aspect of our College life—a level of excellence that will establish Morehouse as one of the best undergraduate, liberal arts

colleges in the nation—one of the best
institutions of any historical tradition, one of
the best, period.

To do so, we dedicate ourselves to 'affirming
excellence at Morehouse'—to a recommitment
to excellence in scholarship, leadership and
service. It is a challenge to which I rise as an
educator, as an alumnus of Morehouse
College, and, now, as its president. Yet,
obviously, it is a challenge I cannot meet alone.

Therefore, let us join together as members of
the Morehouse family, as friends and
supporters of the College, as representatives
of the nation's higher education community—
with the zeal that has sustained this institution
in the past—to embrace the challenge of
propelling Morehouse College into the
future."[223]

On September 18, 1997, President Massey delivered
his memorable speech, "Let Us Praise Famous Men," at the
Fall Convocation. He said,

"All humans are divine...endowed by the
Creator with potential for excellence. Being
famous also means being excellent...At
Morehouse, we have...demonstrated through
the caliber of the men we have graduated...that
ordinary people can do extraordinary things,

143

that the human spirit will triumph over obstacles, that excellence is achievable.

That is what Morehouse is all about ... preparing young men for leadership by providing them with the education, nurture, and support that will enable them to go as far in life as their talents and determination will take them. Given our historic mission and focus on developing leaders, it is no surprise that our list of alumni includes some of the most accomplished men in the world."

Following Massey's exaltation of famous alumni, he turned his attention to the student body:

"All these men came to Morehouse with unrealized potential. They took advantage of offerings at Morehouse. Now, they are famous men. And you can be famous men, too. Look around you, behind you. These Morehouse brothers are tomorrow's lawyers, politicians, and engineers."

Massey concluded his speech by outlining the theme for the academic year:

"Our theme for this academic year is 'Globalizing Excellence: Making Morehouse the Best House.' We must expand our focus to include producing leaders for the global metropolis that the world will be in the 21st century.

I am honored to lead this institution that will
nurture you to excellence. While at
Morehouse, you will be challenged. You are
destined to become famous men—excellent
men—whom the world will one day praise."[224]

On March 2, 1998, President Massey delivered a
speech entitled "Morehouse on the Move" to Morehouse
alumni and invited guests (potential donors) in Los Angeles,
California. He told his audience that "Morehouse is proud of
all of its graduates. They are the tangible evidence of our
historical significance as a great institution." He said,

"Morehouse is on the move, pursuing an
expanded mission to educate leaders. We
graduate more African American men than any
other college or university in the country.
Morehouse produces men who make
significant contributions that benefit
humankind." Finally, President Massey
expressed: "Morehouse men help make the
world a better place. Simply put, when
Morehouse does its job well, the world
benefits."[225]

Lastly, on September 19, 2002, President Massey
delivered his "On Community" speech at the Fall
Convocation. He talked about the value of community at
Morehouse. He stressed one of his favorite themes: the
mandate to rank as one of the best liberal arts colleges in the
country.

145

"In speaking of the Morehouse community, I have often talked about Morehouse as 'World House.' This notion, popularized by Dr. Martin Luther King Jr., a mentee of Howard Thurman, is perhaps the quintessential expression of an open community—a place where we accept and respect *all* others and where, despite our differences, we learn to live together in mutual cooperation and peace. In that regard, I believe that one of our most important functions at Morehouse is to prepare our students to be *world* leaders—to have an impact beyond *any* limited sense of community."

At Morehouse, we strive to develop, maintain and nurture an open, welcoming community that evolves, grows and learns by absorbing the best of other communities, by admitting new people and new ideas, and by allowing challenges – from inside and outside – to existing ideas and traditions. In fact, this kind of openness is the very essence of a learning community, which is precisely what a liberal arts college *ought* to be, and precisely what we say we are.

Our vision for Morehouse is that it will be one of the very best undergraduate liberal arts colleges in the nation—period. This means we want to be one of the very best learning communities in the nation—period. Our goals, then, must include specific strategies and practical processes to ensure that Morehouse becomes just that."[226]

Massey's leadership style was one that "continually identified and communicated the hopes and dreams of the school, thus refocusing and refining the school's purpose and mission."[227] Massey never strayed from his vision: to produce global leaders for the 21st century. Whenever he spoke, he repeated this theme of Morehouse students going out into the world and making a positive impact. In his March 2, 1998, speech to donors, he said, "Simply put, when Morehouse does its job well, the world benefits."[228] In another speech he said, "That is what a Morehouse education is all about—gaining much in terms of knowledge and skills and values—so that you may give much in terms of contributions to the world. You entered Morehouse to learn, you depart to serve."

Dr. Robert Michael Franklin

Dr. Robert Michael Franklin speaking at Commencement, May 20, 2008.
Photo courtesy of Morehouse College, Office of Communications.

The Morehouse Mystique

On July 1, 2007, Dr. Robert Michael Franklin succeeded Dr. Massey as President of Morehouse. Franklin graduated Phi Beta Kappa from Morehouse in 1975 with a Bachelor of Arts degree in political science and religion. He earned a Master of Arts in Christian Social Ethics and Pastoral Care from Harvard Divinity School in 1978 and a Ph.D. in Ethics and Society at the Divinity School, the University of Chicago, in 1985.

At Emory University, Dr. Franklin held posts as a Presidential Distinguished Professor of Social Ethics and a Senior Fellow at the Center for the Study of Law and Religion at the School of Law. He served on the faculties of the University of Chicago, Harvard Divinity School, Colgate-Rochester Divinity School, and Emory University's Candler School of Theology. He served as President of the Interdenominational Theological Center.

Franklin is the author of three books: *Liberating Visions: Human Fulfillment and Social Justice in African American Thought*; *Another Day's Journey: Black Churches Confronting the American Crisis*; and *Crisis in the Village: Restoring Hope in African American Communities*.

On September 20, 2007, Dr. Franklin delivered his first Fall Convocation address to a capacity filled King Chapel audience of students, faculty, staff, alumni, and guests. He articulated his vision that the college must share its repository of "intellectual prosperity" for the benefit of the world.

"My vision is that Morehouse will become a *global resource for educated and ethical leaders*. In our post 9/11 state of affairs, engaging the world with intelligence and

148

integrity is the ultimate ethical *challenge and opportunity*. Working to create a just America is important, but it will be for naught if the rest of the world regards us with contempt because we failed to share our material and intellectual prosperity. In short, this nation and Western civilization need ambassadors who possess and promote enlightenment, integrity and peace predicated upon justice.

These are the very things our greatest and most generous alumnus (Dr. Martin Luther King, Jr.) did as he offered his life in service to others. I am convinced that we can and should pursue this course because it is in our institutional DNA. Morehouse leaders have always been far-sighted and focused on the global arena. From the era of President John Hope's tours abroad to monitor black soldiers in Europe, to Benjamin Mays's service at the World Council of Churches, to Walter Massey's advocacy for peaceful applications of science to global problems, Morehouse has been and should be a force for good both here in 'zip code 30314' and on the far side of the earth."[229]

Dr. Franklin gave his inaugural address to the Morehouse College community on February 15, 2008. He spoke of the need to prepare students as *Renaissance Men with a social conscience.*

"Today, we gather not so much for one person's inauguration as for an institution's academic and moral diagnosis. An inauguration should be a moral checkpoint for all of us to ask, 'Does Morehouse remain committed to the lofty mission that set her course back in 1867? Is Morehouse making good on the ancestors' investments of prayer, money and hope?'

I am here to say today, that thanks to the collective contributions of all of our previous and current stakeholders, Morehouse stands on a firm foundation. Morehouse is as strong as she has ever been, and Morehouse is prepared to march forward as one of the nation's premier liberal arts institutions.

Today, I'd like to declare that Morehouse will prepare 21st century Morehouse Men. And, I'd like to define those Morehouse Men as *Renaissance Men with a social conscience.*

The vision for a Renaissance emerges from listening to Morehouse, feeling Morehouse and walking her sacred grounds for more than 35 years and more intensively during the past eight months. Indeed, my overriding sentiment during the past eight months is that Morehouse is her traditions, her people and her dreams. In fact, we cannot talk about the Morehouse Man as a Renaissance man until we understand the institutional DNA manifest in her traditions, people and dreams."[230]

In an article he wrote for the *National Baptist Voice,* Dr. Franklin reveals that he made the decision to attend Morehouse while watching the funeral of Dr. King on television. At the time, he was a student living on the South side of Chicago. Chicago had not been kind to Dr. King, who had compared the city's climate of hostility, racism, and segregation to the South. In fact, King had called Chicago "the Birmingham of the North." In 1959, the U.S. Commission on Civil Rights had called Chicago "the most residentially segregated large city in the nation."

No doubt this early exposure informed Dr. Franklin's views on leadership development and an important aspect of the vision guiding his Morehouse presidency. In the article, Dr. Franklin advocates a back to basics approach to Black leadership, a return to community. He bemoans the erosion of the Black community and declares that we need leaders who can "restore, even redefine, what membership in that community means."

He states that today's leaders must be expert in the art of reconciliation, mending broken trusts where relationships in the community have failed. While Morehouse, through the leadership of past presidents, has established itself as a world-class institution producing global leaders, Dr. Franklin reminds us that community leadership is still a viable, necessary calling. If African Americans are to be full, active, and productive members of the global community, our own community must aggressively address the issues that have long kept us divided and barred from participation in the national and global arenas.[231]

The Morehouse Mystique

Perspectives of Faculty and Staff

"I help students to set and hold high standards."[232]

Dr. Delores Stephens
Professor, Department of English

Not only is Morehouse a Mecca for Black male students, there is an impressively strong presence of African American male professors on campus. Of the 225 full-time faculty members, *50 percent* are African American men. Overall, 69 percent are male, 31 percent are female. Among part-time faculty, 71 percent are male, 29 percent are female.

Seventy percent of faculty members hold a doctorate: 63 Black males, 21 Black females, 27 "other" males, and 15 "other" females. Thus, African American male professors comprise the largest group of doctorate holders.[233]

There are 371 staff members at Morehouse. Job types are classified as follows: executive/administrative/managerial, professional, technical/paraprofessional, clerical, skilled crafts, and service/maintenance. Most staff members are African American (98 percent) with 47 percent male and 53 percent female.

Mentoring Students

The fourth component of the Morehouse Mystique is the "mentoring of students by faculty and staff." For each generation of Morehouse students, there has been a cadre of faculty and staff who has gone the extra mile to provide unselfish devotion to students. Dr. Mays noted when he assumed the presidency of Morehouse in 1940 that "a few able, dedicated teachers made the Morehouse Man feel that he was 'somebody'…and broadened (students') horizons."[234] Mays challenged his faculty with the following directive: "We must…strive to develop students who have a zeal for learning and who seek knowledge as blind men seek light; and teachers who not only teach, but teachers who inspire students to do their best."[235]

Prominent Morehouse Men of the Mays and Hope eras cited numerous faculty and staff who served as mentors, including but not limited to Samuel Archer, E. Franklin Frazier, Robert Brisbane, Brailsford Brazeal, Melvin Kennedy, E.B. Williams, Addie Mitchell, Anna Grant, Wendell Whalum, James Haines, Henry McBay, Frederick Mapp, and Walter Chivers. Each of these mentors offered hands-on guidance and support to students during pivotal points in their undergraduate careers.

Today the commitment to mentor students lives on through faculty and staff. One such faculty member is Dr. Aaron Parker (class of 1975), Professor of Philosophy and Religion, who likens his role to that of a potter who molds clay into a work of art.

"I wonder at the commencement of another semester whether I will have in my class the scientist who will answer the riddles of sickle cell anemia or acquired immune deficiency syndrome. I ponder at that point, the possibility of intellectually influencing the next playwright…to win the Pulitzer Prize, but to liberate the closed minds of the masses. I think maybe from this class there will emerge a leader of African people and of all people who will speak and work with integrity, providing solutions to critical problems. But I also anticipate touching that student who wants to live a quiet and successful life with his family or local community. This is part of the joy of molding Morehouse Men."[236]

Reginald Davis (class of 1984), an Actuarial Science major and now the Head of the Northern Banking Group of the Wachovia Corporation, has enjoyed the benefits of this molding process. He said his mentor, Dr. Michael Lomax (English professor),

"...seemed to take a general interest in me early on and we have an active friendship that exists to this day. I think it is one of mutual respect, I think he saw something in me perhaps I didn't see in myself. I remember early interactions with him, his prodding in his own way and his encouragement, holding me to a higher standard...."[237]

George Andrews (class of 1974), current President of Capitol City Bank and Trust Company of Atlanta, stated:

"I grew immensely because...the faculty and staff at Morehouse were very supportive and very committed to me obtaining a degree. I'll never forget the warmness, the commitment, and going the extra mile to make sure a Black man did not fall through the safety net, in terms of getting a college degree."[238]

Chapter 8: Perspectives of Presidents,
Faculty, and Staff

Women also serve as mentors. Award winning
filmmaker Spike Lee (class of 1979) credits Dr.
Delores Stephens, his English professor and mentor, for helping to
greatly improve his writing skills.[239] Tommy Brewer (class of
1999) learned an important lesson from Professor Madge
Willis:

"I vividly remember Dr. Madge Willis was one
of the first professors I encountered in my
major field of study. It was a few weeks into
our statistics course and I was developing a
love for psychology. We had come to the point
of our first exam and Dr. Willis caught a
student cheating. Before the entire class, she
confronted the student and told him he had a
choice. He could go to the dean of students or
he could withdraw from the course. She then
said, 'Son, Morehouse Men don't cheat!' I
heard this then and it has since reverberated
in my life as a reminder of my commitment to
integrity. The teachers and staff reinforced high
standards like these and students had to believe
in it. I too believed. I was taught to believe."[240]

Faculty and staff have historically played an important
role in the leadership development of Morehouse students.
Their duties are not limited to teaching knowledge competence
to students; instead, as directed by Presidents Hope and Mays,
they were charged with mentoring, motivating and inspiring
students. Today, prominent alumni credit their success to
faculty and staff going the extra mile for them.

155

The Morehouse Mystique

Views of the Morehouse Experience

Overall, faculty and staff perceived that students are positively affected by their Morehouse experience, and they feel that the experience is unique. Staff members agree with the insights of Andre Pattillo (class of 1979), Director of Athletics:

> "Morehouse is nurturing and has a lot of camaraderie. An experience at Morehouse is the only one that a person can get anywhere; that is, being at a predominantly Black, all-male environment. The reputation of the school makes it unique. It produces a high percentage of leaders in an atmosphere to become a leader, not just to get a job."[241]

Dr. Tobe Johnson said,

> "Many students are very competitive (and) there is a high expectation that the student will achieve. According to social psychologists, the expectation of success is important—the expectation of success breeds success. The single most important thing here (at Morehouse) is the expectation to do well here and not fail when you graduate."[242]

Administration and faculty felt that challenging students made the Morehouse experience meaningful. According to Dean Carter,

"It has a religious tradition that is prophetic, truthful, and powerful. There is an emphasis on students leaving the world better. Morehouse is turning out social engineers with a strong humanitarian perspective."[243]

Dr. Delores Stephens, Chair of the English Department, asserted that:

"It is the only all-male college with a predominantly Black population—that in itself makes it meaningful. Now, many (Morehouse students) have attended predominantly white institutions before college. This experience represents for them the first time that they are in the majority and are the focal group. That makes them grow. Add to this, the alumni, the tradition, the reputation, and the vision of the school."[244]

She added, "We instill in them a sense of responsibility in a non-academic way. We develop in them a sense of responsibility—morally, socially, and behaviorally. We hold them accountable through the syllabus."[245]

Respondents viewed themselves as change agents in the lives of students, whether they served as mentors, advisors, or parental figures. Dean Carter viewed himself as a "counselor, advisor, preacher, college archivist, professor, and chaplain." Cynthia Trawick, Director of the Health Sciences Institute, viewed herself as a "motivator, earnest, realistic evaluator."[246]

The Morehouse Mystique

As we come to the end of this investigation into the success of Morehouse College, we will close with the thoughts and impressions of current Morehouse students in the next chapter.

Chapter 9: Morehouse Students Reflect on their Experience

"These are the best years of my life.
It is great to be in an environment without racism...."[247]
Unidentified Morehouse College Student

Morehouse College attracts some of the best and brightest African American male students from around the country and throughout the world. With a student enrollment of approximately 2,800 students, 98 percent are African American and two percent are Asians, Hispanics, internationals, and whites. Morehouse has a geographically diverse student body, with students coming from approximately 40 states and 35 countries. The largest contingent of students comes from Georgia. California, Texas, New York, and Maryland also send many students. International students come from such wide-ranging countries as the Bahamas, Ghana, India, Japan, South Africa, and Trinidad and Tobago.

Students can choose among 26 majors in the humanities, social and natural sciences, business administration, engineering, and education. The most popular major is business administration, followed by engineering, biology, and political science. With a retention rate of 60.2 percent,[248] Morehouse enjoys one of the highest retention rates among Black colleges and universities in the country.

Every year, approximately 500 students graduate from Morehouse. Most degrees are awarded in business administration, followed by biology and political science. After graduation, a high percentage of Morehouse students enter graduate and professional schools for further study.

The Morehouse Mystique

Among the hundreds of thousands of African American boys who enter elementary school across the United States each year, only a few ultimately graduate from high school. This greatly reduces the pool of young men seeking college admission. The presence of the African American male at mainstream colleges and universities is abysmally low, a national shame. Yet, the ability of Morehouse to attract so many African American men against this backdrop is impressive.

Despite such dire statistics, Morehouse has not lowered its admission standards. The college continues to attract the most academically talented African American male high school students. According to Terrance Dixon, Associate Dean of Admissions at Morehouse, the competition for this "cream of the crop" is akin to the selection process for first round NBA draft picks. Dixon explains, "Everyone wants them."[249] Morehouse's top competitors are the Ivy League schools and other highly selective institutions, including Hampton University, Howard University, Stanford University, the University of North Carolina at Chapel Hill, and Washington University.

One student Morehouse is pursuing is Stephen Michael Eaves, the son of Kevin and Martha Knox. Stephen is a senior in the Science & Technology Program at Charles Hubert Flowers High School in Mitchellville, Maryland. Stephen is an honor student with a 3.3 grade point average. He is vice president of his class, active in the student government association, and a member of the school marching band. Although he received applications from Harvard, Yale, and M.I.T., he decided to apply to Morehouse College, Hampton University, and North Carolina A&T University. He has been accepted and has received scholarship offers to all three schools.

Mr. and Mrs. Knox want their son to attend Morehouse because of the school's legacy of excellence, its reputation for producing professionals, and its focus on developing ethical and politically aware African American men. However, they are weighing the pros and cons of tuition affordability. Stephen would like to attend Morehouse because his grandfather, uncle, and cousins attended. He visited Morehouse during his senior year in high school as part of a Black college tour. He was impressed. He said he liked Morehouse because the "students were serious" and it has an "academic reputation and record of producing prominent alumni."[250]

Views of the Morehouse Experience

According to Associate Dean Dixon, Stephen's reaction to Morehouse is typical. Candidates are impressed by the astuteness of Morehouse students, the strong brotherhood that exists on campus, or just the feeling of the place. For most high school seniors, the campus culture is worlds apart from high school life back home. Dixon says that "approximately 80 percent of those who visit the campus end up enrolling as students."[251]

For some prospective students, that "something they felt" while visiting the Morehouse campus was a spiritual connectedness with like-minded, educated, African American men. Such was the case with Sharif Mitchell (class of 2006):

"Throughout much of my life, I lived in suburban America. I was born in Oakland,

California, relocated for a few years to Miami, Florida, and ultimately moved to Silver Spring, Maryland. Education was valued immensely in my family. My father graduated from New York University, and he received his masters in Hospital Administration from the University of California at Berkeley. My mother received her B.S. in Behavioral Sciences from the University of San Francisco.

I attended private schools from kindergarten to high school and was often the only Black male student. So when I thought of college I always felt the need to be around other Black guys who were ambitious, sharp thinkers, eager to learn, and accepted the fact that it was okay to be an educated Black man in America.

During my junior year at The Maret School, I participated in a college tour of schools in the South and visited Morehouse. It was a spiritual experience for me, because for the first time in my life I got to see the Morehouse brothers interacting outside of the business department wearing suits, talking among each other, fellowshipping and trying to find the good in one another. This really impressed me."[252]

Inspired by the spiritual experience and impressed by the behavior of Morehouse students, Sharif enrolled as a freshman in 2002 and quickly became an active student academically and socially. He was elected president of his junior and senior classes, and he graduated with an Economics degree (with honors) in 2006. Mitchell is now employed as a real estate broker for the prestigious firm of Trammel Crow. The Admissions Office markets the college as a life-altering experience. Associate Dean Dixon says, "Academic excellence and high expectations are the bars. We help students self-select. We look for guys who are motivated, who are balanced, and we look for effort. There is no cuddling at Morehouse."[253]

A perfect example of a student who experienced the life altering effect of Morehouse was Donald Washington, Jr. As a high school junior, Donald was homeless and living in shelters around Washington, DC, with his mother. He had no plans of going to college, but his mom encouraged him, telling him that "he had too much talent not to pursue an education." The vice principal of his high school told him that he looked like a Morehouse Man.

With this encouragement, Donald first attended Montgomery College for three years, and then he applied to Morehouse with a full scholarship offer. When he arrived he lacked confidence, but by his graduation in 2006, he was full of confidence. Washington says, "Before, I was the lamp under the table, but now, I light up the whole room."[254]

Interviews with Morehouse students revealed interesting insights about their experiences. In general, students feel favorable about their college experience, especially their ability to meet academic challenges and the strength of the faculty. They are satisfied that Morehouse is preparing them professionally and personally. They believe the skills they've acquired will lead to success in their future careers and an enhanced sense of responsibility—for themselves, their families, and community. A majority (approximately 82 percent) of the students indicate that the school's academic reputation is the top reason they chose to attend.[255] Family support and the availability of scholarships are other deciding factors.[256]

Personal interviews with students revealed the following sentiments:[257]

"Morehouse gives you tools to make it in life."
"The academic side has been pretty good."
"The people here have changed my life."
"My experience has cleared up self-doubt."
"The networking with students that come from different backgrounds is meaningful."

Virtually all students interviewed indicated that they have experienced personal growth and a strong sense of responsibility. They feel this growth helps them better understand the diverse perspectives of other students. They said,

"I have grown to understand relationships."
"I am more responsible."
"I understand people and think differently due to students."

Students clearly feel that Morehouse is impacting their lives. For example, some students said,

"I don't see myself graduating from another college."
"Morehouse has given me a clearer idea of how to get where I want in life."
"It has made me more responsible and given me a taste of what life is like after graduation."

Chapter 9: Morehouse Students Reflect on their Experience

"I have learned that I am carrying the dreams of my family, so I strive to finish."
"It has not changed my life, but it has given me a clearer idea of how to get there."
"I am a more independent person and more tolerant of gay people."

Students were hard pressed to pin down that one critical, defining moment during their undergraduate career when a transformation occurred. One student said he changed when he received "empathy from his father when he got a sub-par grade." Other shared thoughts were:

"When I was written up for misbehavior, I learned how to handle myself."
"The death of a professor signaled it was time to get serious."
"When I got my girlfriend pregnant, I realized that things had to change."
"After the first semester, I did really well and realized that I could do really well."
"Mentoring at the local elementary school with other Morehouse students changed me."
"The first week of New Student Orientation, Spirit Night was the moment for me."

The aforementioned comments revealed that many students were generally pleased with their Morehouse experience. They treasured the camaraderie and brotherhood among students, and have grown to understand, and appreciate their peers. Students have found their Morehouse experience to be meaningful, though a few have not experienced what they perceive as a critical moment of transformation. Yet overall, students were happy with their decision to attend Morehouse and considered it a special place that is adequately preparing them for their future.

Chapter 10: Epilogue
Concluding thoughts about the Morehouse Mystique

"Morehouse from the onset, even when it was unpopular and even dangerous to do, stressed the education development of the free man and the whole man. Though forced by local law and custom to operate as a segregated institution, Morehouse was never a segregated institution. It was free in a 'slave' culture."[258]

Dr. Edward A. Jones (class of 1926)
Author, *"Candle in the Dark"*

Morehouse College has grown immeasurably in terms of international reputation and influence since being founded in 1867. It is widely respected and admired today for "possessing a unique legacy in the shaping of Black men and Black male leaders."[259] I believe that this reputation is due largely to the prominent alumni who have graduated from the college and have been inspired by the Morehouse mantra aptly described above by Edward Jones.

The Morehouse College experience is more than its curriculum; rather, it can be likened to a comprehensive rites-of-passage-to-living experience where the elders of the academic community receive their sons in embryonic states, provide them with an intensive four-year incubation period of teaching, challenging, mentoring, cajoling, and celebrating; supplemented by an assortment of time-honored traditions, rituals, and ceremonies that mature them toward higher levels of manhood.

Like current students and many alumni, I too am the beneficiary of this transformative experience at Morehouse. While matriculating as a freshman nearly 30 years ago, I experienced my first lesson of the expectations of a Morehouse Man. I vividly remember during the first few days of New Student Orientation I was in line with my Morehouse brothers registering for our fall semester classes. After being distributed the registration forms, I discovered that I did not have a pen to write down my course selection. At the front of the line, however, I saw a faculty member, who I hastily approached and asked if he would loan me his pen. After politely uttering my request, the professor, seizing upon this "teachable moment", intensely looked at me straight in the eyes, and emphatically stated, "Morehouse Men always carry a pen!" His stern words of counsel immediately reverberated within me and have remained until to the present, as I have embraced the habitual practice of "always carrying a pen." Fortunately for me as an impressionable 17-year old, many more lessons were to follow this episode as I learned valuable life-long lessons from professors, coaches, and peers which I apply to my personal and professional life today.

As an educational researcher and practitioner, I am convinced that the Morehouse College formula for success is based partly on its exclusive status as the only all-male, predominately Black college within the American system of higher education, which thereby allows it to provide a tailored academic, cultural, and social institutional culture that has evolved to develop African American males.

Today, the college embraces its historical mission of leadership development and directs much of its resources,

Chapter 10: Epilogue
Concluding thoughts about the Morehouse Mystique

strengths, and energies towards its fulfillment. Many time-honored traditions, rituals, and ceremonies have been maintained with the singular purpose of exalting, enlightening, and empowering African American male students into leaders. Among these, I believe that the most enduring, effective, and important tradition from the late 1880s through the early 1960s has been Chapel, which grew out of the theological origins of the school, but ceased to be defined as theologically Christian under Dr. Benjamin Mays, who developed the assembly into a matrix for the holistic development of Morehouse Men. The greatest benefit of Chapel—now referred to as Crown Forum—is that it provides a common denominator experience for students to become indoctrinated with the moral and intellectual values and ideals espoused by the college.

Finally, Peterson and Deal assert that all schools over time "develop a unique personality, cope with tragedies, and celebrate successes."[260] Morehouse College in its evolutionary progression from the humble origins in the basement of the Springfield Baptist Church in rural Augusta to its current designation as one of "the best schools in America for African Americans" is indeed a cause for celebration. The unique personality of Morehouse, however, is not so much the result of internal tragedies, but it is the result of a collective reaction to external realities of how African American men have historically been portrayed and victimized in America.

Yet, evidence from its solid record of graduating many alumni of national and international acclaim, producing the most baccalaureate degrees for African American males than any other college or university, and its consistent production of many professionals Morehouse demonstrates that it has a proven formula for success that is worthy of emulation by other educational institutions in America and abroad.

Footnotes

[1] Benjamin E. Mays, *Born to* Rebel: *An Autobiography* (Athens, GA: University of Georgia Press, 1971), p. 172.

[2] Jacqueline Fleming, *Blacks in College: A comparative study of students' success in black and white institutions* (San Francisco, CA: Jossey-Bass Publishers, 1984), p.170.

[3] Ibid, p. 170.

[4] Leslie Miller-Bernal "College Experiences and sex-role attitudes: Does a women's college make a difference?" *Youth and Society,* June, 1989. Cornelius Riodan, "Single and mixed-gender colleges for women: Educational, attitudinal, and occupations outcomes," *Review of Higher Education.* Spring, 1992. Cornelius Riodan, "The value of attending a women's college: Education, occupation, and income benefits," *Journal of Higher* Education, July/August, 1994. Daryl G. Smith, "Paths to success: Factors related to the impact of women's colleges," *Journal of Higher* Education, May/June, 1990.

[5] Alexander W. Astin, *What matters in college? Four critical years revisited* (San Francisco, CA: Jossey- Bass Publishers, 1993). Fleming, *Blacks in College,* 1984.

[6] Addie L. Butler, *The Distinctive College: Talladega, Tuskegee, and Morehouse* (Metuchen: NJ: The Scarecrow Press, 1977). Jacqueline Fleming, *Blacks in College,* 1984.

[7] Charles J. McDonald, Morehouse College, Candle in the Dark Gala, Award Acceptance Speech, February 19, 2005.

[8] "Reaching across generations at Morehouse College," *Journal of College Science Teaching*, February, 1997, p. 251.

[9] *A Gathering of Men Reunion*, Morehouse College publication, 1998, p. 11.

[10] "Toping the List," *Morehouse College Outpacing the Competition*, Morehouse College publication, circa. 2005, p. 1.

Footnotes

11 "Morehouse Still #1 in Educating the Best and Brightest," *Morehouse College Outpacing the Competition*, Morehouse College publication, circa. 2005, p. 1.

12 Morehouse College website, 2008.

13 "Wall Street Journal Ranks Morehouse Among the Top Feeder Schools," *Morehouse College Outpacing the Competition*, Morehouse College publication, circa. 2005, p. 1.

14 Elizabeth L. Ihle, "Black women's education in the south: The dual burden of sex and race," In J. Antler, & S.E, Biklen, *Changing education: Women as radicals and* conservators (New York, NY: State University of New York Press, 1990), pp. 89-106.

15 David Hefner, "Where the boys aren't," *Black issues in higher education,* June 17, 2004, pp. 70-75.

16 Admissions Viewbook, Morehouse College publication, 1996.

17 Lerone Bennett, Jr. "Celebrating Black Male Excellence," *Ebony,* June, 1992, p. 34.

18 Kevin Chappell, "Reverse Integration," *Ebony,* May, 1998, p. 65.

19 G. Glenn, "Following the leaders: Leadership development becomes priority for many institutions," *Black Issues of Higher Education,* March 7, 1997, p. 22.

20 Clayborne Carson, "Martin Luther King, Jr.; The Morehouse Years," *The Journal of Blacks in Higher Education,* Spring, 1997, p. 124.

21 Edward A. Jones, *A Candle in the Dark: A History of Morehouse College* (Valley Forge, PA: Judson Press, 1967), p. 10.

22 "We have come a long way," *90 Years of Building Men,* Morehouse College, 1957, p. 3.

23 "Educating Theologians," *Harper's Weekly Newspaper*, April 13, 1867, p. 238. In *African American History in the Press: From the coming of the Civil War to the Jim Crow as reported and illustrated in selected newspapers of the time,*

the Schneider College (Detroit, MI: Gale Publishers, 1996), pp. 510-511.

[24] Ibid., p. 510.

[25] *"The Southern Commanders,"* Harper's Weekly, *April 6, 1867, p. 218.* In *African American History in the Press: From the coming of the Civil War to the Jim Crow as reported and illustrated in selected newspapers of the time, the Schneider College* (Detroit, MI: Gale Publishers, 1996), p. 510.

[26] Benjamin Brawley, *History of Morehouse College* (College Park, MD: McGrath Publishing Company, 1970), p. 25.

[27] Ibid., p. 27.

[28] John Hope, Morehouse College 50th Anniversary Address, *The Standard*, 1917. Retrieved from the Robert W. Woodruff Library, Atlanta University Center, Special Archives/ Collection.

[29] Jones, *A Candle in the Dark,* p. 316.

[30] Brawley, *History of Morehouse College*, p. 53.

[31] Ibid., p. 56.

[32] Brawley, *History of Morehouse College,* p. 56.

[33] Ibid., p. 68.

[34] Ibid., pp. 80–81.

[35] Ibid., p. 10.

[36] Ibid., p. 83.

[37] Ibid., pp. 100–101.

[38] Morehouse College Brochure, undated from the early 1900s, p.1. Retrieved from the Auburn Avenue Research Library, Samuel H. Archer Private Collection.

[39] John Hope, "Morehouse College and Negro Education after Fifty Years," The Standard, March 10, 1917, p.6. Retrieved from the Robert W. Woodruff Library, Atlanta University Center Archives/Special Collection.

[40] Mark S. Giles, "Howard Thurman: The Making of a Morehouse man, 1911-1923." Retrieved on June 15, 2008 from the Education Foundations Website.

[41] Hope, "Morehouse College and Negro Education After Fifty Years," *The Standard*, March 10, 1917, p. 2.

[42] W.E.B. DuBois, "The Talented Tenth," from *The Negro Problem: A Series of Articles by Representative Negroes of Today*, New York, 1903.

[43] John Hope, "Negro Education in the United States" speech, Tenth Annual Conference of I.S.S., Mount Holyoke College, 1931, p.3. Retrieved from the Robert W. Woodruff Library, Atlanta University Center, Archives/Special Collection.

[44] James D. Anderson, "Training the apostles of liberal culture: Black Higher Education, 1900-1935," In L.F. Goodchild, & H.S. Wescheler, (Eds). *The ASHE reader on the history of higher education.* (Needham, MA: Ginn Press, 1989).

[45] "Life and works of John Hope, 1868-1936," *Atlanta University Bulletin*, 1936, p. 18. Retrieved from the Robert W. Woodruff Library, Atlanta University Center Special Collections/Archives.

[46] S. Milton Nabrit, "Morehouse in Science, 1921-1932," *Morehouse Alumnus*, Vol. V, No. 2, December, 1932, p. 2.

[47] "A Gathering of Men," *Morehouse College Reunion* (brochure), 1998, p. 11.

[48] *Morehouse College Bulletin*, 1945, p. 2.

[49] Mays, *Born to* Rebel: An Autobiography, p. 91.

[50] John Hope Exhibit, Morehouse College Archives.

[51] *Morehouse College: A Liberal Arts College for Men*, Morehouse College publication, 1933, p. 2.

[52] Leroy Davis, Jr., *John Hope of Atlanta: Race leader and Black educator* (Unpublished dissertation, Kent State University, 1989), p. 139.

[53] Ibid., p. 139.

[54] Howard Thurman, *With Head and Heart: The Autobiography of Howard* Thurman (New York, NY: Harcourt Brace Jovanovich, 1979), p. 36.

[55] Ibid., p. 36.

⁵⁶ Ibid., p. 36.

⁵⁷ *The Torch*, Morehouse College Yearbook, 1923, p. 3.

⁵⁸ John Hope Exhibit, Morehouse College Archives.

⁵⁹ Thurman, *With Head and Heart: The Autobiography of Howard Thurman,* p. 86.

⁶⁰ Ibid., p. 37.

⁶¹ *Morehouse Alumnus*, November, 1931, Vol. 4, No. 2, p. 5.

⁶² *Morehouse College: A Liberal Arts College for Negro Men*, 1933, p. 2.

⁶³ *The Morehouse Alumnus*, Vol. XVI, No. 39, November, 1948. p. 18.

⁶⁴ Jones, 1967, p. 108.

⁶⁵ David Morrow, "The Morehouse College Glee Club," *The Western Journal of Black Studies*, Vol. 11, No. 4, November 4, 1987, pp. 181.

⁶⁶ Ibid., "The Morehouse College Glee Club," 1987, pp. 181–184.

⁶⁷ Thurman, *With Head and Heart: The Autobiography of Howard Thurman,* p.35.

⁶⁸ Ibid., p. 35.

⁶⁹ The Torch, Morehouse College Yearbook, 1923, p. 106.

⁷⁰ Mordecai Johnson exhibit, Morehouse College Archives.

⁷¹ Giles, p. 2.

⁷² Ibid., 2007, p. 2.

⁷³ The Torch, Morehouse College Yearbook, 1923, p. 47.

⁷⁴ Thurman, p. 40.

⁷⁵ The Torch, Morehouse College Yearbook, 1923, p. 42.

⁷⁶ Jones, *A Candle in the Dark: A History of Morehouse College,* 1967, p. 235.

⁷⁷ Morehouse College Brochure, undated from the early 1930s, p.3.

⁷⁸ *The Atlanta University Bulletin*, Series III, No. 15, July, 1936, pp. 3–4.

Footnotes

79 *Morehouse College: A Liberal Arts College for Negro Men*, 1933.

80 Thurman, p. 38.

81 Ibid., p. 37.

82 *Bulletin of Morehouse College*, January, 1940, Vol. 9, No. 12. pp. 14-15.

83 *The Atlanta University Bulletin*, July, 1931, p. 6.

84 "Dr. John Hope is awarded 1935 Spingarn Medal posthumously as recognition of leadership," *The Atlanta Bulletin*, July, 1936, Series III, No. 15, p. 2.

85 Benjamin E. Mays, "We drive towards the stars," *Alumnus Magazine*, The President's Page, Morehouse College, Vol. XIII, 1944.

86 Benjamin Mays exhibit, Morehouse College Archives.

87 Benjamin E. Mays, "Opening Chapel Service Welcome Speech," *The Morehouse Alumnus,* Bulletin of Morehouse College, Vol. 10, No. 15, February 1941, pp. 6–7.

88 *The Morehouse Alumnus*, The President's Page, Vol. XVIII, No. 46, July, 1950, p. 10.

89 John H. Eaves, "Speakers of the House: Morehouse Men Reflect on their Journey to Manhood (Atlanta, GA: Publishing Associates, 2006), p. 256.

90 Beth Gallasby, "The Man Morehouse Built," *The Beaumont Enterprise News*, February 19, 2006, p. 4-A.

91 *The Morehouse Alumnus*, Morehouse College Bulletin, Vol. XIII, No. 27, March–April, 1945.

92 Benjamin Mays Exhibit, Morehouse College Archives.

93 Mays, *Born to Rebel,* p. 179.

94 Eaves, 2006, p. 170.

95 Eaves, p. 140.

96 *Maroon Tiger*, October 1942, p. 1.

97 Eaves, p. 105.

[98] Benjamin. E. Mays, "I don't mind getting beat, but—," The President's Page, *Morehouse Alumnus*, Vol. XXIV, No. 70, November, 1956, p. 19.

[99] Mays, *Born to Rebel,* p. 191.

[100] Eaves, p. 170.

[101] Ibid., p. 32.

[102] *The Alumnus*, Morehouse College Bulletin, Vol. XXIV, No. 70, November, 1956, p.19.

[103] Eaves, p. 170.

[104] Benjamin E. Mays, "Challenge to Graduating Class of 1958," *Alumnus,* "Morehouse College Bulletin, July, 1958, Vol. XXVI, No. 77.

[105] Benjamin Mays Exhibit, Morehouse College Archives.

[106] *Alumnus*, Morehouse College Bulletin, The President's Page, 1944.

[107] Mays, *Born to Rebel,* p. 172.

[108] Benjamin E. Mays, "Twenty-Seven Years of Success and Failure at Morehouse," Centennial Commencement Address, Morehouse College, *The Morehouse College Bulletin*, Summer, 1967, p. 32.

[109] Interview with Michael L. Lomax, President/CEO of the United Negro College Fund, March 14, 2005.

[110] "Mays Radio Address," given by Dr. Benjamin E. Mays on WGST Radio, Atlanta, GA, February 18, 1946, *Morehouse Alumnus*, April, 1946, p. 6.

[111] Mays, *Born to Rebel,* p. 265.

[112] Martin Luther King, Jr. "The Dimensions of a Complete Life" speech, April 9, 1967, New Covenant Baptist Church, Chicago, Illinois.

[113] Martin Luther King, Jr., "Chapter 2: Morehouse College," *The Autobiography of Martin Luther King, Jr.*, Retrieved, December 31, 2008. http://www.stanford.edu/group/King/publications/autobiography/chp_2.htm.

Footnotes

[114] Ibid. http://www.stanford.edu/group/King/publications/autobiography/chp_2.htm.

[115] Mays, *Born to Rebel,* p. 265.

[116] Clayborne Carson, *"Martin Luther King, Jr.: The Morehouse Years," The Journal of Blacks in Higher Education,* Spring, 1997, p. 125.

[117] Martin Luther King, Jr., "Chapter 2: Morehouse College," *The Autobiography of Martin Luther King, Jr.,* Retrieved, December 31, 2008. http://www.stanford.edu/group/King/publications/autobiography/chp_2.htm.

[118] Interview with Judge Horace T. Ward, U.S. Federal Judge, May 31, 2006.

[119] Eaves, *Speakers of the House: Morehouse Men Reflect on their Journey to Manhood,* p. 105.

[120] Carson, Luker & Russell, eds., *The Papers of Martin Luther King, Jr. Volume I: Called to Serve, January 1929–June 1951,* University of California Press, 1992.

[121] "The Purpose of Education," *The Maroon Tiger,* Student Newspaper, January-February, 1947.

[122] Christine King Farris, "King, the Morehouse Years (1944–1948): An Intimate Conversation with those who knew him best," a panel discussion held at **Morehouse College,** April 1, 2008.

[123] June Dobbs Butts, "King, the Morehouse Years (1944–1948): An Intimate Conversation with those who knew him best," a panel discussion held at **Morehouse College,** April 1, 2008.

[124] Carson, Luker & Russell, eds., *The Papers of Martin Luther King, Jr. Volume I: Called to Serve, January 1929-June 1951* (University of California Press, 1992).

[125] Farris, "King, the Morehouse Years (1944–1948): An Intimate Conversation with Those Who Knew Him Best," **Morehouse College,** April 1, 2008.

[126] Lerone Bennett, Jr., *What Manner of Man: A Biography of Martin Luther King, Jr. 1929-1968* (Chicago, IL: Johnson Publishing Company, Inc. 7th ed, 1989), p. 34.

[127] "The Achievements of Morehouse Men in the Great Universities," Morehouse College undated publication circa. 1950, p. 3.

[128] Ibid, p.3.

[129] Biography of Mordecai Wyatt Johnson, King Encyclopedia, retrieved on June 14, 2008, from the King Encyclopedia Website.

[130] Mays, *Born to Rebel,* p. 268.

[131] Ibid., p. 274.

[132] Eaves, *Speakers of the House: Morehouse Men Reflect on their Journey to Manhood,* p. 31.

[133] Ibid., p. 358.

[134] Ibid., p. 359.

[135] Interview with Congressman Sanford Bishop, February 1, 2005.

[136] Eaves, *Morehouse Men Reflect on their Journey to Manhood,* p. 150.

[137] "Maynard H. Jackson," *Notable Black American Men: Narrative biographical essays of 500 prominent African-American men from historical to contemporary times*, (1998) edited by Jessie Carney Smith. p. 603.

[138] Robert Michael Franklin, "Let us make Man," Founders' Day Inauguration Address, February 15, 2008.

[139] Walter R. Allen, "The Color of Success: African American college student outcomes at predominately white and historically black public colleges and universities," *Harvard Education Review,* 1992. Walter R. Allen & Nesha Z. Haniff, "Race, gender, and academic performance in U.S. higher education," In W.R. Allen, E. Epps, & Haniff, Nesha .Z. (Eds.)

College in black and white: African American students in predominately white and in historically black public universities (pp.95-109), 1991. Alexander Astin, Minorities in American Higher Education (San Francisco, CA: Jossey-Bass Publisher, 1982). Jacqueline Fleming, *Blacks in College* (San Francisco, CA: Jossey-Bass Publishers, 1984). Michael Nettles, "Racial similarities and differences in the predictors of college student achievement." In W.R. Allen, E. Epps, & Nesha Z. Haniff, (Eds.), *College in black and white: African American students in predominantly white and in historically black public universities* (New York, NY: University of New York Press, 1991), pp. 75-91). Ernest T. Pascarella, "College environmental influences on learning and cognitive development: A critical review and a synthesis." In J.C. Smarth (ed), *Higher education handbook of theory and research.* (New York, NY: Agatha Press, 1985), pp. 1-61.

[140] Pascarella, 1985.

[141] Astin, 1982, pp.91–92.

[142] Patricia Gurin & Edgar Epps, *Black consciousness, identity, and achievement: A study of students in historically black college.* (New York, NY: John Wiley & Sons, 1975).

[143] Leslie Miller-Bernal "College experiences and sex-role attitudes: Does a woman's college make a difference?" *Youth and Society,* June, 1989, p. 363-387. Leslie Miller-Bernal "Single-sex coeducational environments: A comparison of women students' experiences at four colleges," *American Journal of* Education. 1993, pp. 23-54. Cornelius Riodan, "Single and mixed gender colleges for women: Educational, attitudinal, and occupational outcomes," *Review of Higher Education*, 1992, Spring, pp. 486-510. Cornelius Riodan (1994, July/August), "The value of attending a women's college: Education, occupation, and income benefits," *Journal*

of Higher Education, pp. 486-510. Jacqueline Fleming, *Blacks in College,* 1984.

144 Kevin Bushweller, "Separate by choice," *The American School Board Journal,* October, 1996, pp. 34-37. Ronnie Hopkins, *Educating Black males* (New York, NY: State University of New York, 1997). Ronald Mincy, "Nurturing Black males," (Washington, DC: The Urban Institute Press, 1994).

145 Kevin Bushweller, "Separate by choice," *The American School Board Journal,* October, 1996, pp. 34-37.Ronnie Hopkins, *Educating Black males* (New York, NY: State University of New York, 1997). Ronald Mincy, "Nurturing Black males," (Washington, DC: The Urban Institute Press, 1994).

146 Addie Butler, *The Distinctive Black College: Talladega, Tuskegee, and Morehouse* (Metuchen, NJ: The Scarecrow Press, 1977), p. 100.

147 Mays, p. 172.

148 David Hefner, "Where the boys aren't," *Black Issues of Higher Education,* June 17, 2004, p. 70.

149 Ibid., p. 72.

150 Jerlando F.L. Jackson & James Moore III, "African American males in education: Endangered or ignored?" *Teachers College Record,* February, 2006, p. 201.

151 *"One in 100: Behind Bars in America 2008,"* The Pew Center on the States, (Washington, D.C.: Pew Charitable Trust Report, 2008), p. 5.

152 Darryl Bailey & Pamela O. Paisley, "Developing and nurturing excellence in African American male adolescents," *Journal of Counseling & Development,* Winter, 2004, p. 11.

153 *One in 100: Behind Bars in America 2008,* pp. 3, 34.

154 Bruce Western, Vincent Schiraldi, & Jason Ziedenberg, "Education and incarceration," *Policy Report* (Washington, D.C: Justice Policy Institute, 2003), p. 6.

Footnotes

[155] U.S. Department of Justice Statistics, 2008.

[156] Pedro A. Noguera, *The Trouble with Black Boys: An Other Reflections on Race, Equity, and the Future of Public Education* (San Francisco, CA: Jossey-Bass Publishers, 2008).

[157] Bailey & Paisley, p. 11.

[158] Ibid., p. 5.

[159] Antoine M. Garibaldi, "Educating and motivating African American males to succeed," *Journal of Negro Education*, Journal of Negro Education, Winter, 1992, v61 n1 p. 4-11. Courtland Lee, "Empowering young black males," (Ann Arbor, MI: ERIC Clearinghouse on Counseling and Personnel Services, No. ED 341 1887), 1991.

[160] Rinku Sen (2006), "*A Positive Future for Black Boys: Building the Movement*, (Cambridge, MA: The Schott Foundation for Public Education), p. 3.

[161] Western, Schiraldi, & Ziedenberg, 2003, p. 6.

[162] Luebchow Lindsey, "Minority recruitment: Athletics success, admissions failure," January 24, 2008. Retrieved on June 7, 2008 on *The Higher Education Watch* website blog.

[163] Jawanza Kunjufu, *Countering the Conspiracy to Destroy Black Boys* (Chicago, IL: Afro-American Publishers, 1983).

[164] James Comer, "Quotations from James Comer," *School Power*, ch. 2, 1980. Retrieved from Poem.Hunter.com website.

[165] Sakita Holley, "Gender ratio: More than 2:1," The Hilltop, The Daily Student Voice of Howard University, September 10, 2007. Retrieved on June 22, 20008 on the Hilltop Online, The Daily Student Voice of Howard University website.

[166] Benjamin E. Mays, "WGST radio address on 78th Anniversary of Morehouse College," February 1946, Morehouse College Bulletin, Vol. XIII, No. 27, March-April, 1945. p. 2.

[167] Terrence E. Deal & Kent E. Peterson, *Shaping school culture* (San Francisco, CA: Jossey-Bass, 2002), p.10.

168 Jones, p. 10.
169 Mays, p. 173.
170 Benjamin E. Mays, "Centennial Commencement Address: Twenty-seven years of success and failure at Morehouse," *The Morehouse College Bulletin*, Summer, 1967, p. 31.
171 Fleming, p. 50.
172 Interview with Betty Burney, August 7, 2007.
173 Giles, p. 1.
174 Eaves, 2006, p. 184.
175 Ibid., p. 68.
176 Robert Michael Franklin, "Facing the Rising Sun" speech, Morehouse College, September 20, 2007.
177 Robert Michael Franklin, "Facing the Rising Sun," speech, Sept. 20, 2007.
178 Eaves, 2006, p. 160.
179 Eaves, p. 160.
180 Eddie Gaffney interview, January 27, 2005.
181 Admissions Viewbook, Morehouse College, p. 5.
182 Ibid., p. 5
183 Giles, p. 9.
184 Eaves, 2006, pp. 144–145.
185 Ibid., p. 183.
186 Ibid., p. 183.
187 Ibid., p. 42.
188 Ibid., p. 104.
189 Ibid., p. 68.
190 Ibid., p. 58.
191 Ibid., p. 25.
192 Ibid., p. 90.
193 Ibid., p. 79.
194 Ibid., p. 184.
195 Merriam Webster's New Collegiate Dictionary, 5th ed, 1977, p. 739.
196 Michael Lomax interview, March 14, 2005.

Footnotes

[197] Walter E. Massey, New Student Convocation Address, Morehouse College, August 18, 1997.

[198] Admissions Viewbook, 1996, p. 6.

[199] Robert Michael Franklin, "Presidential Charge to Graduates," Morehouse College, May 18, 2008.

[200] Admissions Viewbook, 1996, p. 11.

[201] Eaves, 2006, p. 184.

[202] Ibid., p. 184.

[203] Anthony Harris, "What is a Morehouse Man?" *Maroon Tiger*, Morehouse Student Newspaper Op-ed, 2007.

[204] Butler, p. 100.

[205] Ibid., pp. 100-101.

[206] Kent D. Peterson & Terrence E. Deal, *The Shaping School Culture* Fieldbook," (San Francisco, CA: Jossey-Bass, 2002), p. 39.

[207] Jennie Rasband, "Rituals and rites of passage, celebrations: A social resource for elementary teachers," Fall, 1996. Retrieved on June 15, 2008 from the Utah State University website.

[208] Robert Michael Franklin, "President's Charge to Graduates," Morehouse College, May 18, 2008.

[209] Lerone Bennett, Jr. interview, New Century Capital Campaign Video, Morehouse College, 2006.

[210] John H. Eaves, "Demystifying the Morehouse Mystique: Determining which factors lead to the academic success of African American college students at the nation's only predominantly Black all-male college," unpublished dissertation (Columbia, SC: University of South Carolina, 1999), p. 81.

[211] Admission V*iewbook*, 1996, p. 1.

[212] Jan Collins-Eaglin & Stuart A. Karabenick, "Devaluing of academic success by African American students: On

'Acting White' and 'Selling Out.'" Paper presented at the Annual Meeting of the American Educational Research Association, Atlanta, GA, 1993.

[213] Peterson and Deal, p. 35.

[214] Stacy Grayson interview, New Century Campaign Video, 2006.

[215] John Wilson, student testimonial. Retrieved from the Morehouse College Website, February 16, 2005.

[216] Interview with Benjamin Spencer, February 22, 2005.

[217] George Kuh, and others, *Involving Colleges: Successful approaches to fostering student learning and development outside the classroom* (San Francisco, CA: Jossey-Bass, 1991).

[218] Lemuel Watson & George Kuh. "The influence of dominant race environments on students' involvement, perceptions, and educational gains," *Journal of College Student Development*, July/August, 1996, pp. 415-424.

[219] Patricia Gurin & Edgar Epps, *Black consciousness, identity, and achievement: A study of students in historically black colleges* (New York, NY: John Wiley and Sons, 1975).

[220] Walter E. Massey, "President's Charge to Graduates" address, Morehouse College, May 17, 1998.

[221] Walter E. Massey, Inauguration Address, Morehouse College, February 16, 1996.

[222] Walter E. Massey, "President's vision," Morehouse College Website, 2005.

[223] Walter E. Massey, "Inauguration Address" speech, February 16, 1996.

[224] Walter E. Massey, "Let us praise famous men" speech, September 18, 1997.

[225] Walter E. Massey, "Morehouse on the Move" speech, March 2, 1998.

[226] Walter E. Massey, "On Community" speech, September 19, 2002.

[227] Deal and Peterson, p. 89.

[228] Walter E. Massey, "Morehouse on the move," speech, March 2, 1998.

[229] Robert Michael Franklin, "Facing the Rising Sun: A New Day Begun" speech, **September 20, 2007.**

[230] Robert Michael Franklin, "Let Us Make Man ...Morehouse Man," The Inauguration Address, Morehouse College, February 15, 2008.

[231] Robert Michael Franklin, "Coretta Scott King: Reflections on the Funeral and the Future of the Movement." Retrieved from Emory University website: www.candler.emory.edu as published with permission of the *National Baptist Voice.*

[232] Delores Stephens interview, May 19, 1998.

[233] Morehouse College Fact Book, 1998–2003 (Atlanta, GA: Office of Institutional Research, Morehouse College, September, 2004), p. 26.

[234] Mays, p. 173.

[235] Benjamin Mays Exhibit, Morehouse College Archives.

[236] Aaron L. Parker, "The Joy of Molding Morehouse Men," *Morehouse College Update*, Office of Public Relations, June, 1990, p. 12.

[237] Eaves, p. 82.

[238] Ibid., pp. 25–26.

[239] Ibid., p. 117.

[240] Ibid., p. 37.

[241] Interview with Andre Pattillo, May 19, 1998.

[242] Interview with Tobe Johnson, June 5, 1998.

[243] Interview with Lawrence Carter, May 7, 1998.

[244] Interview with Delores Stephens, May 19, 1998.

[245] Interview with Delores Stephens, May 19, 1998.

[246] Interview with Cynthia Trawick, May 19, 1998.

[247] John H. Eaves, Demystifying the Morehouse Mystique, unpublished dissertation, 1999, p. 95.

[248] 1998–2003 Fact Book, Morehouse College, p. 20.

[249] Terrance Dixon interview, January 17, 2004.

[250] Stephen Michael Eaves interview, November 20, 2005.

[251] Terrence Dixon interview, January 17, 2004.

[252] Eaves, 2006. p. 128.

[253] Terrence Dixon interview, January 17, 2004.

[254] Errin Hayes, "Morehouse graduates largest class ever," Associated Press, May 20, 2006. Retrieved from CBS News website, June 15, 2008.

[255] Eaves, 1999, p. 82, (tabulated results from a consortium report from the CIRP Freshman Survey, 1997).

[256] Ibid., p. 82.

[257] Excerpts of standardized interviews conducted for dissertation research, "Demystifying the Morehouse Mystique" during the 1997-1998 academic year at Morehouse College.

[258] Jones, 1967, p. 225.

[259] Giles, 2007, p. 1.

[260] Peterson & Deal, p. 9.

References

Admissions Viewbook. (1996). Atlanta: Morehouse College (brochure).

A Gathering of Men, Reunion 1998. (1998). Atlanta: Morehouse College (brochure).

Alumnus: The Morehouse College Alumni Magazine. (2002). 59(1), Atlanta: Morehouse College.

Allen, W.R. 1987, (May/June). Black colleges vs. white colleges: The fork in the road for black students. *Change,* 19(3), pp. 28-34.

Allen, W.R. (1988, Summer). Improving Black student access and achievement in higher education. *Review of Higher Education,* 11(4), pp. 403-416.

Allen, W.R. (1992). The color of success: African American college student outcomes at predominantly white and historically black public colleges and universities. *Harvard Education Review,* 62(1), pp. 26-43.

Allen, W.R., & Haniff, N.Z. (1991). Race, gender, and academic performance in U.S. higher education. In W.R. Allen, E. Epps & N.Z. Haniff, (Eds.), *College in black and white: African American students in predominantly white and in historically black public universities* (pp. 95-109). New York: University of New York Press.

Anderson, J.D. (1989). Training the apostles of liberal culture: Black higher education, 1900-1935. In L.F. Goodchild, & H.S. Wescheler, (Eds.), *The ASHE reader on the history of higher education* (pp. 455-477). Needham, MA: Ginn Press.

Astin, A.W. (1982). *Minorities in American higher education.* San Francisco: Jossey-Bass Publishers.

Astin, A.W. (1993). *What matters in college? Four critical years revisited.* San Francisco: Jossey-Bass Publishers.

Bailey, D.F., & Paisley, P.O. (2004, Winter). Developing and nurturing excellence in African American male adolescents, *Journal of Counseling & Development*, Vol. 82, pp. 10-17.

Bailey, D.F. (2004). Developing and nurturing excellence in African American male adolescents. *Journal of Counseling & Development*, 82(1), pp. 10-16.

Bennett, L. (1989). Martin Luther King, Jr.: A biography (7th ed). Chicago: IL: Johnson Publishing Company, Inc.

Bennett, L. (1992, June). Celebrating Black male excellence: Morehouse College renews commitment on 125th anniversary. *Ebony,* 47(8), pp. 26-34.

Biography of Mordecai Wyatt Johnson, Retrieved June 14, 2008, from King Encyclopedia Website http:// www.stanford.edu/group/King/about_king/encyclopedia/ johnson_mordecai.html.

Bonner, F.A. (2003, Spring). To be young, gifted, African American and male, *The Gifted Child Today*. 26(2), pp. 26-34.

Bowles, F., & DeCosta, F.A. (1971). *Between two worlds: A profile of Negro higher education.* New York: McGraw-Hill Company.

Brawley, B. (1970). *History of Morehouse College.* College Park, GA: McGarth Publication Company.

References

Bressler, M., & Wendell, P. (1980, November/ December). The sex composition of selective colleges and gender differences in career aspirations. *Journal of Higher Education,* 51(6), pp. 650-663.

Bushweller, K. (1996, October). Separate by choice. *The American School Board Journal,* 44(1), pp. 34-37.

Butler, A.L. (1977). *The distinctive college: Talladega, Tuskegee, and Morehouse.* Metuchen, NJ: The Scarecrow Press.

Carson, C. (1997, Spring). Martin L. King Jr.: The Morehouse years. *The Journal of Blacks in Higher Education,* 5(3), pp. 121-125.

Carson, Luker & Russell, eds., *The Papers of Martin Luther King, Jr. Volume I: Called to Serve, January 1929- June 1951,* (University of California Press, 1992) Carson, ed., *The Autobiography of Martin Luther King, Jr.* (New York: Warner Books, 1998).

Centennial Commencement: 1867-1967 program (1967). Atlanta: Morehouse College.

Chappell, K. (1998). Reverse integration: White student blends in a Black college. *Ebony, 53*(7), pp. 64-68.

Chenoworth, K. (1998), July 8. The surging degree wave. *Black Issues in Higher Education, 15*(1), 20-22, pp. 43-48.

Collins-Eaglin, J. & Karabenick, S.A. (1993, April). Devaluing of academic success by African American students: On "Acting White" and "Selling Out. Paper presented at the Annual Meeting of the American Educational Research Association, Atlanta, GA.

CIRP Freshman Survey. (1997). Higher Education Research Institute. Los Angeles: UCLA College? Where are the Black males? Retrieved on June 22, 2008 on Black Excel website: http://www.blackexcel.org/ratios.htm.

Coulotta, E. (1992, November 13). Black colleges cultivate scientists. *Science, 258*(5085), pp. 1216-1218.

Davis, L. (1989). *John Hope of Atlanta: Race leader and Black educator.* Unpublished doctoral dissertation, Kent State University.

Davis, J.E. (1994, Fall). College in black and white: Campus environment and academic achievement of African American males. *Journal of Negro Education,* 63(4), pp. 620-633.

Dawson-Threat, J. (1997, Winter). Enhancing in-class academic experiences for African American men. *New Directions for Student Services*, Vol. 80, pp. 31-41.

Deal, T.E & Peterson, K.D., (2002). *Shaping school culture.* San Francisco: Jossey-Bass.

DeSousa, D.J. & Kuh, G. (1996). Does institutional racial composition make a difference in what black students gain from college? *Journal of College Student Development,* 37(3), pp. 257-267.

Douglas, W. (1983, December 4). Men of the house: What's this Morehouse mystique that stays through life? *The Atlanta Journal-Constitution*, pp. 1-F, 7-F.

DuBois, W.E.B. (1902). The talented tenth. *The Negro Problem: A Series of Articles by Representative Negroes of Today*, p. 41.

References

Eaves, J. (1999). "Demystifying the Morehouse Mystique: Determining which factors lead to the academic success of African American College students at the nation's only all-male, predominantly black post-secondary institution," Unpublished dissertation, The University of South Carolina, Columbia, SC.

Eaves, J. (2006). Speakers of the House: Morehouse Men Reflect on their Journey to Manhood. Atlanta: Publishing Associates.

Educating Theologians, Harper's Weekly Newspaper, April 13, 1867. *African American History in the Press: From the coming of the Civil War to the Jim Crow as reported and illustrated in selected newspapers of the time, the Schneider Collection.* (1996). Detroit: Gale, pp. 510-511.

Fleming, J. (1984). *Blacks in college: A compara-tive study of students' success in black and white institutions.* San Francisco: Jossey-Bass Publishers.

Footsteps: African American History Magazine. (2001, November/December). Charles Baker, ed. Peterborough, NH: Cobblestone Publishing Company.

Franklin, J.H. (1980). *From slavery to freedom: A history of Negro Americans*, (5ᵗʰ ed.). New York: Alfred Knopf.

Franklin, R. M. (2007, September 20). *Facing the rising sun,* Fall Convocation speech. Retrieved on May 10, 2008 from the Morehouse College Website: www.morehouse.edu.

Franklin, R. M. (2008, February 15). *Let us make man,* Founders' Day, Inauguration address. Retrieved on May 10,

2008 from the Morehouse College Website: www.morehouse.edu.

Gallaspy, B. (2006, February 19). *The Man Morehouse Built*. The Beaumont Enterprise News (Beaumont, TX), pp. 1-A, 4-A.

Garibaldi, A.M. (1992). Educating and motivating African American males to succeed. *Journal of Negro Education,* 61(1), pp. 5-11.

Giles, M. (2007, Winter). Howard Thurman: The making of a Morehouse man, 1911-1923. Retrieved on June 15, 2008 from the Education Foundations Website: http://findarticles.com/p/articles/mi_qa3971/is_200701/ai_n18705844.

Glenn, G. (1997, March 7). Following the leaders: Leadership development becomes priority for many institutions. *Black Issues in Higher Education,* 14(1), pp. 22-25.

Gurin, P., & Epps, E. (1975). *Black consciousness, identity, and achievement: A study of students in historically black colleges.* New York: John Wiley and Sons.

Harris, A. What is a Morehouse Man? Retrieved on June 15, 2008 from the Morehouse College Maroon Tiger website: http://www.morehouse.edu/themaroontiger/opinions/archives/001086.html. .

Hayes, E. (2006). Morehouse graduates largest class ever. Retrieved on June 14, 2008 from the CBS News website: (http://www.cbsnews.com/stories/2006/05/20/ap/national/mainD8HNLOMG0.shtml.

References

Hefner, D. (2004, June 17). Where the boys aren't. *Black Issues of Higher Education.* 21(9), pp. 70-75.

Holley, S. (2007, September 10). Gender ratio: More than 2:1. Retrieved on June 22, 2008 on The Hilltop Online, The Daily Student Voice of Howard University, website: http:/ /media.www.thehilltoponline.com /media/storage/paper590/news/2007/09/10/LifeStyle/ Gender.Ratio.More.Than.21-2958818.shtml.

Hope, J. (1917, March 10). Morehouse College and Negro Education after fifty years, *The Standard,* p. 6.

Hope, J. (1931). *Negro Education in the United States* speech, Tenth Annual Conference of I.S.S., Mount Holyoke College.

Hopkins, R. (1997). *Educating Black males.* New York: State University of New York Press.

Ihle, E.L. (1990). Black women's education in the south: The dual burden of sex and race. In J. Antler, & S.K. Biklen, *Changing education: Women as radicals and conservators* (pp. 89-106). New York: State University of New York Press.

Jackson, J.F.L. & Moore, J.M. (2006, February). African American males in education: Endangered or ignored? *Teachers College Record.* 108(2), pp. 201-205.

Johnson, R.E. (1993). *Factors in the academic success of African American college males.* Unpublished doctoral dissertation, University of South Carolina at Columbia.

Jones, E.A. (1967). *A candle in the dark: A history of Morehouse College,* Valley Forge, PA: Judson Press.

Kuh, G, Schuh, J., Whitt, E., Andreas, R., Lyons, J., Strange, C. Krehbiel, L., & MacKay, K. (1991). *Involving colleges: Successful approaches to fostering student learning and development outside the classroom.* San Francisco: Jossey-Bass.

King, M.L. (1947, January-February). The purpose of education. *Maroon Tiger*, Atlanta: Morehouse College.

Kunjufu, J. (1983). *Countering the conspiracy to destroy black boys.* Chicago: Afro-American Images.

LaVeist, T., & Whigham-Desir, M. (1999, January). Colleges for African Americans. *Black Enterprise,* 44(1), pp. 71-80.

Lee, C. (1991). *Empowering young black males.* (ERIC Clearinghouse on Counseling and Personnel Services, Ann Arbor, No. ED 341 1887).

Lloyd, R. G (1992, January-April). The plight of Black males in America: The Agony and the ecstasy-A summary comment. *Negro Educational Review,* 43(1-2), pp. 41-44.

Luebchow, L. Minority recruitment: athletics success, admissions failure. Retrieved on June 7, 2008 on The Higher Education Watch website blog, January 24, 2008.

Mays, B.E. (1941, February), "Opening Chapel Service" welcome speech, *The Morehouse College Bulletin,* Vol. 10, No. 15, pp. 6-7.

Mays, B.E. (1967, Summer), "Centennial Address: Twenty-seven years of success and failure at Morehouse College, *The Morehouse College Bulletin,* pp. 29-32.

References

Mays, B.E. (1971). *Born to rebel: An Autobiography.* Athens, GA: University of Georgia Press.

Mercer, J. (1998, February 13). Walter Massey, a classic Morehouse man, seeks to add to his institution's luster. *The Chronicle of Higher Education,* 44(23), pp. A49-50.

Merriam Company (1977). *Webster's New Collegiate Dictionary.* (5ᵗʰ ed.). Springfield, MA: G & C Merriam Company.

Miller-Bernal, L. (1989, June). College experiences and sex-role attitudes: Does a women's college make a difference? *Youth and Society,* 20(4), pp. 363-387.

Miller-Bernal, L. (1993). Single-sex coeducational environments: A comparison of women students' experiences at four colleges. *American Journal of Education,* 102(1), pp. 23-54.

Mincy, R. (1994). *Nurturing Black males.* Washington, DC: The Urban *Institute Press.*

More about the house. (1998, September). Atlanta: Morehouse College (newsletter).

Morehouse at a glance. (2008). Atlanta: Morehouse College (brochure).

Morehouse College: A liberal arts college for Negro men. (1933) Atlanta: Morehouse College (brochure).

Morehouse College Fact Book. (1997-2003). Office of Institutional Research, Atlanta: Morehouse College.

Morehouse College update. (1990, June). Atlanta: Morehouse College (newsletter).

Morehouse Outpacing the Competition. (2005). Atlanta: Morehouse College publication.

Morrow, D. (1987) The Morehouse College Glee Club, *The Western Journal of Black Studies*, 2(4), pp. 181-184.

Nabrit, M. (1932, December). Morehouse in Science, 1921-1932, *Morehouse Alumnus,* 5(2), p. 16.

Nettles, M. (1991). Racial similarities and differences in the predictors of college student achievement. In W.R. Allen, & E. Epps, & N.Z. Haniff, (Eds.), *College in black and white: African American students in predominantly white and in historically black public universities* (pp. 75-91). New York: University of New York Press.

Noguera, P.A. (2008). The Trouble with Black Boys: And Other Reflections on Race, Equity, and the Future of Public Education, 1st ed. San Francisco: Jossey-Bass Publishers.

Notable Black American Men: Narrative biographical essays of 500 prominent African-American men from historical to contemporary times, (1998) *Maynard H. Jackson,* Jessie Carney Smith (ed), p. 602.

One in 100: Behind bars in America 2008. (2008). The Pew Center on the States. Washington, D.C.: The Pew Charitable Trusts.

Quotations from James Comer. Retrieved on June 22, 2008 from website: Poem Hunter.Com. Quotations from James Comer, http://www.poem_hunter.com/quotations/famous.asp?people=_James%20P%20Comer. (James P. Comer (20th century), U.S. psychiatrist and author. School Power, ch. 2 (1980).

References

Pascarella, E. (1985). College environmental influences on learning and cognitive development: A critical review and a synthesis. In J.C. Smarth (ed.), *Higher education handbook of theory and research* (pp.1-61). New York: Agatha Press.

Perkins, L.M. (1989). The impact of the 'Cult of the True Womanhood" on Education of black women. In *ASHE reader: The history of American higher education* (pp. 154-159). Needham, MA: Ginn Press.

Peterson, K.D. & Deal, T.E. (1999). *The Shaping School Culture Fieldbook.* San Francisco: Jossey-Bass Publishers.

Phillip, M., & Morgan, J. (1993, December 16). The Morehouse mystique: A proud tradition of producing great men, *Black Issues in Higher Education,* 10(1), pp. 16-19.

Rasband, J. (1996, Fall). Rituals and rites of passage, Celebrations: A Social Resource Guide for Elementary Teachers, College of Education. Retrieved on June 15, 2008 from the Utah State University website: http://teacherlink.ed.usu.edu/tlresources/units/Byrnes-celebrations/Rites%20of%20Passage.html.

Reaching across generations at Morehouse College, (1997, February), *Journal of College Science Teaching,* pp. 250-252.

Riodan, C. (1992, Spring). Single and mixed-gender colleges for women: Educational, attitudinal, and occupational outcomes. *Review of Higher Education,* 15(3), pp. 327-346.

Riodan, C. (1994, July/August). The value of attending a women's college: Education, occupation, and income benefits. *Journal of Higher Education,* 65(4), pp. 486-510.

Roebuck, J.B., & Murty, K.S. (1993). *Historically Black Colleges and Universities: Their place in American higher education.* Westport, CT: Praeger.

Scales, A.M. (1992, January-April). Focus on the African American males: A Response. *Journal of Negro Educational Review,* 43(1-2), pp. 22-27.

Sen, R. (2006) A positive future for Black boys: Building the movement, The Schott Foundation for Public Education, Cambridge, MA.

Slater, R.B. (1994, Spring). The Blacks who first entered the world of white higher education, *Journal of Blacks in Higher Education,* 2(4), pp. 47-56.

Smith, D. (1990, May/June). Paths to success: Factors related to the impact of women's colleges. *Journal of Higher Education,* 66(3), pp. 245-266.

The Atlanta University Bulletin. (1936, July). 15(3), Atlanta: Atlanta University.

The many paths to success. (1997, February). *Journal of College Science Teaching,* 26(4), pp. 247-252.

The Morehouse Alumnus. (1930, November), 1(3), Atlanta: Morehouse College.

The Morehouse Alumnus. (1931, November), 2(4), Atlanta: Morehouse College.

The Morehouse Alumnus. (1932, December), 2(5), Atlanta: Morehouse College.

References

The Morehouse Alumnus: Bulletin of Morehouse College. (1936, November). 6(1), Atlanta: Morehouse College.

The Morehouse Alumnus: Bulletin of Morehouse College, (1938, January). 7(5), Atlanta: Morehouse College.

The Morehouse Alumnus: Bulletin of Morehouse College, (1939, May). 8(11), Atlanta: Morehouse College.

The Morehouse Alumnus: Bulletin of Morehouse College, (1940, January). 9(12), Atlanta: Morehouse College.

The Morehouse Alumnus: Bulletin of Morehouse College, (1941, February). 10(15), Atlanta: Morehouse College.

The Morehouse Alumnus: Bulletin of Morehouse College. (1943, November). Vol. XI, Atlanta: Morehouse College.

The Morehouse Alumnus, (1944, March-April). Vol. XII, Atlanta: Morehouse College.

The Morehouse Alumnus, (1945, July-August). Vol. XIII, Atlanta: Morehouse College.

The Morehouse Alumnus, 1945, March-April. Vol. XIII, Atlanta: Morehouse College.

The Morehouse Alumnus: Bulletin of Morehouse College, 1948, May. 16(39), Atlanta: Morehouse College.

The Morehouse Alumnus: Bulletin of Morehouse College, 1950, July. 18(46), Atlanta: Morehouse College.

The Morehouse Alumnus: Bulletin of Morehouse College, 1956, May. 24(70), Atlanta: Morehouse College.

The Morehouse Alumnus: Bulletin of Morehouse College, 1964, May. 32(101), Atlanta: Morehouse College.

The sudden drop to college completion by African Americans. (1997/1998, Winter). *Journal of Blacks in Higher Education, 5*(2), p. 19.

The Torch: Morehouse College Yearbook. (1923). Atlanta: Morehouse College.

Thurman, H. (1979). *With Head and Heart: The Autobiography of Howard Thurman.* New York: Harcourt Brace Jovanovich.

Top fifty colleges for Black students. (2003). Retrieved on June 14, 2008 from the Black Enterprise Magazine website: (http://www.infoplease.com/ipa/A0771723.html).

U.S. Department of Justice Statistics, Retrieved on June 7, 2008 on the U.S. Department of Justice Website: http://www.ojp.usdoj.gov/bjs/welcome.html.

Washington, V, & Newman, J. (1991). Setting our own agenda: Exploring the meaning of gender disparities among Blacks in higher education. *Journal of Negro Education, 60*(1), pp. 19-35.

Washington, C.M. (1997). A study of early academic performance, attrition, and retention as related to selected cognitive, non-cognitive, and adjustment variables for African American college students attending a private, open admission, historically black institution. (Doctoral dissertation, University of South Carolina, 1997).

Watson, L.W., & Kuh, G.D. (1996, July/August). The influence of dominant race environments on students' involvement, perceptions, and educational gains: A look at historically Black and predominantly White liberal arts institutions. *Journal of College Student Development, 37,* 415-424.

We have come a long way: 90 years of building men, Morehouse College brochure (1957), p. 3.

Western, B, Schiraldi, V, & Ziedenberg, J. (2003), Education and incarceration, *Policy Report,* Washington, DC: Justice Policy Institute.

Williams, L. (1987). Molding men: At Morehouse College middle class blacks are taught to lead. *The Wall Street Journal*, pp. 1, 25.

Notes